DIVORCED
on the Redneck Riviera

Ms. Linnie Delmar

authorHOUSE®

AuthorHouse™
1663 Liberty Drive
Bloomington, IN 47403
www.authorhouse.com
Phone: 1-800-839-8640

First published by AuthorHouse 9/13/2010

ISBN: 978-1-4520-4340-1 (sc)
ISBN: 978-1-4520-4341-8 (hc)
ISBN: 978-1-4520-4342-5 (e)

Library of Congress Control Number: 2010912308

Printed in the United States of America

This book is printed on acid-free paper.

About the Author

Ms. Linnie Delmar has been a Licensed Massage Therapist for more than twenty-five years and continues to own and operate a day spa out of her home in Fairhope, Alabama.

The dedication and exceptional talent that separate her from all the rest have taken her around the world and given her the opportunity to work with A-list actors and more than ten motion-picture production companies. Her clients have included such celebrities as Gene Hackman, Steven Seagal, Geraldo Rivera, Merle Haggard, the singing groups Backstreet Boys and Alabama, Major Ronald Ferguson, B. B. King ... the list goes on and on. All had interesting stories to tell.

Linnie Delmar has also had four husbands, and she will tell you how she met and fell in love with each of them and how they fell in love with her. Each was unique and had a story to tell. One was a workaholic, one was an alcoholic, one turned out to be gay, and one was an actor/addict hooked on pain pills. Linnie tells it like it is, and she uses humor to mask her pain over losing each of them.

This is the story of Linnie's life as she tells it, through her eyes as she saw it, from her heart as she felt it, and through her free-spirited soul as she lived it to the fullest. "Never a dull moment" has always been her motto. Reading this book will reveal that she is like a female Forrest Gump, in the right place at the right time all through her life. Her stories haven't always had happy endings, but ultimately, she found her place of serenity and happiness.

Foreword

This book is dedicated to all the good women and men in the world who seek that one special person who will look at them and say the three little words they have waited a lifetime to hear. Not *I love you*—a trite and token phrase we use carelessly day in and day out, sometimes for real and sometimes not. No, the three words we long to hear are *You're the one*: "You're the one I want to be my lover, my best friend, my soul mate, and I want to spend the rest of my life with you—just you."

It is also dedicated to the good women and men who may never hear those words but are happy and content with their families, friends, and pets. What more can a person want than to be happy and complete in their own right, alone? We don't need another person to complete us. Love that is given out of a complete soul is the most fulfilling love of all.

This is Linnie Delmar's story and her journey to find out how to be content and serene. You may learn something about your life from this account of her life. She had lessons to learn, but she kept failing the final test. The guidance kept coming until she finally got it.

That's how the universe works. It keeps sending experiences until the lesson is accepted. Learn how she saw the signs but ignored them and kept getting married again and again. She is a good Southern woman and did everything in her power to make her marriages work ... except pick the right man.

Most of all, find out how this happened to a smart, attractive, fun-loving Southern girl who always knew better. She saw all the warning signs but ignored them. She allowed physical desire to disguise that still small voice that tells us a mistake is on the way. After many mistakes, that small voice grew louder and louder until Linnie finally listened. This book was written with the hope that you will learn to listen to *your* inner spirit and find the strength to celebrate your uniqueness.

This is Linnie's story in her own words. Her story may inspire you, it may amuse you, but it will never bore you. Some of the names were changed to protect the guilty.

Table of Contents

Prologue

THE AWAKENING

I call it "the awakening" because it wasn't until after I turned sixty that the truth hit me like a ton of bricks, and I finally woke up to the real world I lived in and not "Linnie's World," a pretend world of finding the perfect life and the perfect man to share it with. My past life was like ashes in the wind before my moment of clarity.

Before I tell you the story of my life from the beginning, I want to tell you about my life as it is today. I lead a very simple life, one that some people would find dull by today's standards. I'm here to tell you that it's anything but that!

I own a very small business here in Fairhope, Alabama. I'm a Licensed Massage Therapist (LMT), and each day is an eye-opener about the world and the people who live in it. You will find out as you read the book that I have traveled around the world working on a lot of people who all have interesting stories, including celebrities like Gene Hackman, Merle Haggard, and Steven Seagal. Because of my work with A-list actors and famous musicians, I have been labeled Massage Therapist to the Stars. I continue to work with more than ten motion-picture production companies and enjoy the travel and the unique business of making movies.

You will also find out that I have had four husbands along my journey of life. I want you to know why, despite all the red flags and signs not to marry these men, I did it anyway. I want everyone, especially women, to pay attention to that small but familiar voice inside or that gut feeling that always tells you something is right or wrong. Listen to it very closely. My vision and hunger to find that perfect fairy-tale life with the perfect man to complete me as a person and complete us a couple was what I thought I was meant to do to in today's society, but it wasn't.

Now, with the gift God has given me—a unique massage technique that separates me from all the others—I fulfill my soul and my spirit with joy and happiness. Words can't begin to express how whole I feel as the person I have become today. Just to be here to help and pamper people like you is an epiphany every day. Today was no exception. My first client arrived at nine-thirty in the morning.

"My name is Jason. I ... I have a gift certificate for a ... massage."

I could tell by his hesitation that this was his first massage experience. "Go ahead into the changing room. I will get you an information form to fill out."

Jason confirmed my suspicion when he hesitantly told me, "This is my first time to get a professional massage." He seemed very nervous.

"I promise it won't hurt a bit," I jokingly told him.

But he was so nervous he didn't get the joke. "Oh, I know it won't. I didn't mean that."

As he went into the treatment room, I went into the separate changing room to look at the information form he had filled out. I read that he was only twenty-one. I also saw that his clothing was folded and neatly placed on the chair. I could tell right away that Jason must be in the military because of the perfection with which he had folded his clothing.

When I went in to begin my treatment on Jason, he confirmed my belief that he was in the military. "I get deployed to Afghanistan tomorrow," he told me. Such a terrible war that was claiming so many of our strong young men, I thought. I could tell in his voice, however, that Jason was proud to be a soldier and he had no fear going into this unknown, God-forsaken country. At that point, I knew young Jason was not only my new best friend, but someone I admired and looked up to as well.

As always, I was going to do my best and give Jason a massage experience he wouldn't soon forget. As I got into working my magic techniques on Jason, I could feel the muscles start to relax and the positive energy coming from his warm body through my hands.

"Jason," I instructed, "remember this moment. Remember how warm you are, like being enclosed in a cocoon. Remember, as well, the smells of all the oils and European lotions that have been used on your body. Most of all, remember how soft this table is and how you feel like you are sinking into it, completely calm and relaxed. Tuck this very moment into your mind's eye so that when you can't sleep, this thought will be in your memory as vivid as it is right now." I asked him to turn over on his stomach for me to complete his massage. I always start with my clients on their back.

When I completed the treatment, Jason said, after a few moments, "I am so relaxed, I can barely stand and walk. I don't remember ever being this relaxed." Before Jason left, I asked him if he remembered what I told him, and he looked me in the eye and said, "Miss Linnie, I will never forget what you told me, and I will never forget you." With tears in my eyes, I told him that it had been an honor and a privilege to work on him and give him his very first professional massage. He then left.

I could hardly wait for him to get out the door before I broke down crying and asking God to please bring this strong, wonderful kid back home safe to his parents and his loved ones. It is days like this that complete me as the person I am today. I see how far I have come in my circle of life and what my future will be tomorrow! It's the simple stories like this that I hold so dear to my heart, and it's what makes me cherish people like Jason. I am able to help them deal with the stress that plagues our society and people's complicated lives. It also makes me be a better person each and every time I meet a person like Jason. It turns my life into the best life I could ever ask for, because in a very small way, I want to believe I can make a difference in their lives as much as they have made a difference in mine.

Chapter 1

THE PATH BEGINS AT
A BROKEN HOME

The tempests in my life began with my birth, which maybe was a foreshadowing of things to come. I was born after a very long, hard labor involving many back-breaking hours and lots of pain. Isn't that the same story every mother tells about labor?

I was finally delivered by a young navy doctor. I wasn't breathing at all and had turned completely blue. They all thought I was dead. This young intern was determined that his first delivery wasn't going to die. He performed mouth-to-mouth resuscitation until I began to breathe on my own. Mama was screaming in horror, not knowing if I was dead or alive. She was a nervous wreck.

The young doctor made a big mistake and mentioned to Mama that I had already turned blue before he brought me back to life. From that day forward, every mistake I ever made was blamed on me being born a blue baby. If I have heard it once, I have heard it a million times. She would say in a low whisper, "You know, after all, she was born a blue baby." To this day, I still don't want to believe what I think it means. Of course, the way Mama says it, I am led to believe that since I was born a blue baby,

I'm not the brightest bulb in the box; I'm one brick shy of a full load or one goose shy of a gaggle. I have always been called the pretty one while my other two sisters are called the smart ones. Since the day I was born, I have been trying to prove to Mama that her blue baby can be both pretty and smart, just like her.

Before my parents met and had me, they already had interesting stories of their own. My mother, a true Southern lady in every respect, is from Mobile, Alabama, and my biological father is a Yankee from Akron, Ohio. Other than both of them being very attractive, smart, and blessed with the most beautiful blue eyes you will ever see, they had nothing in common.

She had an adventuresome soul. The first real job she got was as a secretary at the Pentagon in Washington, D.C, where she was one of the youngest interns ever hired. She had no idea at the time that she was working in one of the largest buildings in the world. She was always late for work because she got lost every day trying to find her office—all the hallways looked the same. She took it upon herself to take her roller skates to work to wear so that she could find her office faster. Her boss was so impressed that he told her it was okay and to tell the other ladies that they could do the same in order for all of them to be on time for work. She started a trend that continued the entire time she worked there.

As a shy Southern transplant, she had many thrilling experiences. One of the best was visiting New York City and being in Times Square when it was announced that the Korean War was over. Everyone started kissing in the streets. I can see her now with her natural blonde hair, those exquisite blue eyes, a high-fashion outfit, and high heels, loving every minute of it.

Mom and Dad met at a skating rink when he was stationed in Pensacola, Florida. Both of them were accomplished skaters since childhood. He fell hard for her Southern charm and natural beauty.

When he was transferred to San Francisco, he begged her to follow him out there. With the same adventurous spirit that had led her to Washington, D.C., she agreed to move to the West Coast. It was a long train ride away. When her worried family sent her off, her grandma gave her one hundred dollars and told her, "You be careful of those strange people on that train." She followed Grandma's advice and pinned her money on the outside of her bra. But she fell asleep during the night and woke to find her money gone. Someone took her money right out of her bra. She was out of her environment and totally broke. What a mess! A nice navy man came to her rescue and loaned her a dollar to make a phone call to Dad so that he could come pick her up at the train station.

My mom and dad were married in beautiful San Francisco in 1945 by the same justice of the peace who, in later years, married Marilyn Monroe and Joe DiMaggio—in the same building, even the same room. How romantic was that?

After that exciting start, they moved to depressing Akron, Ohio, the rubber capital of the world and site of the home offices of the Goodyear and Firestone tire companies. My parents rented a small one-bedroom apartment that, in no time, Mama made into a charming home for the both of them. On a windy day, the smell of rubber was in the air to the point that it made Mama sick sometimes. It was very cold with lots of snow in Akron. Because Mama was raised on the warm, beautiful Gulf Coast of Mobile, she hated the cold so much. She felt cold most of the time and really disliked the snow. She was so homesick. She missed her mother and father and the warm sunshine and Southern hospitality of Alabama.

Because my dad was gone so much working, Mama suffered from extreme loneliness and depression. All she thought about was having a baby, a wish that was realized in 1948—after a move to Portsmouth, Virginia—with my dramatic birth on the navy base. They moved into a two-bedroom apartment that she made into the perfect little nest to bring me home to. I was the only grandchild on my dad's side of the family, so I was spoiled by my granny and by my mom and dad. My mama made most of my beautifully detailed baby clothes. My granny gave me a gold necklace and bracelet that I wore every day, and she liked to dress me up as often as possible.

At age four, I was so tired of being an only child and lonely, I kept bringing kids home from our neighborhood. I begged Mama to get me a baby sister. Finally, my beautiful baby sister Valerie was born. I was so happy because, even though I was only four years old, I wanted to care for her and protect her as a big sister should. This is a recurring theme in my life—taking care of others. To this day, my sister is still very important to me; she's a huge part of my life.

Val and I slept in the same tiny bedroom together, and after Mama would put us to bed, I would climb into Val's baby bed, pull her out, and put her in my bed with me to keep her warm and safe. I held her as close as I could to my tiny little body. I changed her diaper and dressed her in her finest outfit.

We had cement floors in our tiny two-bedroom apartment. Mama still talks about how I was able to carry around my baby sister and never drop her. She also told me how, from the early age of four, she knew I was different. I would have Val dressed in a uniquely different outfit every day. I always loved dressing up, and I made sure Val was dressed to the nines every day too! To this day, I still love dressing up and changing clothes, with a fresh new look and hairstyle and makeup to match each outfit.

From an early age, I was always neat, tidy, and organized. I would make sure all of our toys were put away and our bedroom was shipshape each night before we went to bed. I also had a habit from a very young age of giving some of my toys, clothes, and household goods to friends and neighbors.

This habit continues to this day, because it makes me feel so good inside to share anything I have and give away anything I think someone might need.

These were the first signs Mama noticed of the ADD and OCD that would cause me lots of problems in school and in my adult life. The OCD, which my friends see as a blessing of being organized and sharing, turned into a real positive attribute in my career as an LMT in my adult years. Details are so important, and I don't overlook any—especially when I am doing a massage treatment on my clients.

When I was just getting used to having a baby sister to love and take care of, my mama decided to divorce my dad. Mama planned to leave and move back to Mobile, to live with her mother and father. Valerie was just six months old. Mama couldn't stand any more cold weather, but most of all, she had had enough of my father being so jealous and insecure and very hard to get along with. My family life and the world as I knew it were about to change.

All of this made me feel so sad, and it was very hard for me to understand why my mama wanted to leave my dad and not take him with her. But the worst was yet to come.

The night before the big move back to Mobile, Mama told me she was not able to take *me* with her.

"Honey, I can't take you with me," my mother said that night. "I have to work. Nanny and Grandpa can take care of Valerie, but you are too active. They can't keep up with both of you at the same time."

I can remember so well how sad and scared I felt that night. If my mama and my beloved baby sister were going away from my dad, why did *I* have to stay with my dad? As an adult, I totally understand why she did what she had to do. She had no money, no job, and no place to live other than with her parents. She had no choice other than to leave me behind. At four years old, though, I was thinking I would never see them again.

"Why can't I go?" I begged.

"You just can't. I am so sorry. I explained it to you." Maybe she did, but it didn't make sense to me.

It broke my heart to see the moving van drive away. I screamed and cried, "Please don't leave me, Mama," as she took my baby sister and waved good-bye. I thought they were gone forever.

The next day, my dad and I moved into a damp two-bedroom basement apartment with his mother, who managed the large apartment building.

Granny was so happy to have us move in with her. She loved the fact that my dad could be her handyman at the apartment building. Dad worked full-time at the Goodyear Tire Company, but in his spare time he was Mr. Fixit for the tenants. I was alone all day with my granny.

Granny turned out to be the best grandmother I could have ever wished for. Each and every day I could feel her love for me, and I loved her right back. I had all her of her attention, and I loved her dearly now more than ever. She was a good role model for me at that age, and I knew she would never leave me like Mama did.

"I love you, baby," she would say, and I knew she meant it. The problem was that I missed my mama and my baby sister so terribly that I was sad and depressed all the time. I was so miserable that I couldn't eat and had trouble sleeping. Because of this heartbreak, I was often sick during the two years I lived with Granny. I was so thin, frail, and weak. I had multiple earaches and bad colds most all the time.

My granny would rock me to sleep so many cold nights, blowing warm air in my ears to stop the continuous pain. Without her love and concern, I think I might have died—not only from being so sick but also from loneliness and misery from missing Mama and my baby sister, Val.

Being from a broken home started a pattern that was set for me for the rest of my life. Mama had four husbands later in her life. I, too, would have four husbands in my adult life as well.

At age four, though, all I wanted was to have my family together again like it was before—me and my baby sister, Val, in the tiny two-bedroom apartment Mama had made into a warm, cozy home for us.

It wasn't long after Mama left that my dad remarried, but I still stayed with granny. Granny and I would play games together. The best game of all was playing house and having real tea parties. We would use her finest china and crystal, because somehow she always knew that I would never drop or break anything. I was always so careful and organized while putting things back in their proper place, like she had taught me to do. My granny also taught me good manners. She was a beautiful woman who loved me with all her heart.

My new stepmother, who also worked full-time at Goodyear like my dad did, acted like she hated me and saw me as an inconvenience, but that was through the eyes of a four-year-old. On the other hand, my granny saw me as nothing but a joy that had come into her life. My dad was an only child, and Granny was thrilled to have me, telling me often, "Child, you're the greatest blessing I could have in my old years." I felt warm, safe, and loved every time she held me close to her.

My stepmother never had any children and was much older than my dad. In later years, she tried her best to be nice to Valerie and me because we were nice to her. We always knew she didn't really love us. She did love my dad though and, to this day, is a wonderful wife to him. I thank God that he has her and they have each other and are totally devoted to each other. I have tried to keep in touch with both of them through the years, but they don't want to be a part of my life or Val's. They have made that very clear to us. That's their loss, and we have done all we can to love them throughout the years.

Finally, after two long years, my mama came to Ohio to get me and take me to my real home in Mobile, Alabama. I was six and Val was two years old. It was the best day of my young life, knowing I would have my family together again. Mama had married again, and her new husband, Arnold (we named him Papa), was the perfect man for Mama and perfect stepdad for Val and me in every way. From the first time I met him, I could feel the love! He and Mama had gone on a honeymoon to Niagara Falls, and I thank God they came by to pick me up on the way back to Mobile. When Mama saw me, her first comment was how skinny and pitiful I looked. I did look like a tiny sad little skinny person who needed a lot of love and healing after being away from my mama and baby sister for so long. I cherished the thought of having my family with me each and every day. God, I was glad to see them. I had been in a car wreck at age six with my dad and had lost most of my teeth. But teeth or no teeth, I felt like a million dollars, and I couldn't get that big goofy smile off my tiny little face!

Papa was so good to his two new stepdaughters! He was by far the coolest man I have ever seen. He was six feet two inches tall and about one hundred seventy-five pounds. He was extremely good-looking and a sharp dresser from head to toe. His shoes always looked new and were always shined. His clothes were always starched and ironed. He was soft-spoken, and best of all, he was rich! Mama had married well, and finally we could have the life she wanted us to have thanks to Papa! He was in every sense of the word a true Southern gentleman and a Christian man who loved to read the Bible to us as often as possible. He taught us the true value of life and how to have a loving family.

He also loved music and played the harmonica while Mama played the piano. They always drove new Cadillacs, one for him and one for her. We also had a summer home on the Little Lagoon in Gulf Shores, Alabama, where we spent every summer. We always had a big boat to ski behind and a smaller boat to shrimp with. Papa made sure we knew how to swim, ski, and drive a boat at a very young age because we lived on the water in the summertime. Papa did everything he could do to spoil all the women in his life.

Papa owned a huge grocery store in Mobile. I loved the idea of never having to pay for anything. When we went there, I would always load up with candy when Mama wasn't looking. Since I was the ringleader and it was free, I would always get enough candy for Val and my brand new baby sister, Kim, and of course, a lot for me, too. I have always had a sweet tooth.

Now that I was ten years old, Kim was like my real-life baby doll. Just like I wanted to do with Val, it was my job to protect and take care of both of them, and if I do say so myself, I did a darn good job! I taught both of them how to organize their bedrooms and keep them as clean as our full-time maid, Miss Sealy, did. One year for Christmas, Mama and Papa made the mistake of buying me huge chalkboard. I thought to myself, *I will enforce and instruct my sisters how to properly organize and clean their rooms the right way.* I wanted their rooms to look like mine, which was perfect. The problem was, they had no signs of having OCD. It was like pulling teeth to get them to think like me, doing it the Linnie way. At age ten, I thought my way was the only way. With them fighting and screaming the whole time, I taught them the proper skills to clean their rooms. I would give it the white-glove test and then grade them. They hated that and probably hated me for making them do it. I would give them a grade from one to ten, with ten being the best grade they could get, which wasn't very often. One time I made the mistake of going behind Miss Sealy and giving her a grade of eight instead of a ten, and of course I was wearing my famous white glove. To say the least, the next day my chalkboard was thrown to the curb, and I never found the white glove again. That ended my days of being the best drill sergeant I could be to my beloved sisters.

I also taught them how to perform in a talent show and not be shy by singing and dancing each Sunday after church for Mama and Papa. We would stand on the brick fireplace hearth that was raised up like a stage and sing, dance, and show off any talent that I would tell them to do—always with my help and supervision, of course.

From an early age, I never liked following the usual rules, so I would make up my own set of rules for my sisters and me. My set of Linnie's Rules also applied to all my cousins, especially Wanda, Debbie, and George Ann, who stayed with us a lot. They too did everything I told them to do. Of course, I stayed in trouble with Mama most of my life—she always knew that if something went wrong, it was my fault. After all, I was the blue baby.

Mama did throw me a crumb every so often and give me a compliment. She told everyone how good I was about going up to anyone and starting a conversation. She said that I talked to people as if I had known them for years, because I loved people so much. To this day, I have never met a stranger I didn't like.

"You also have the nerve of Dick Tracy," she always said ... whatever the hell that meant! Of course, the way she said it made me feel like I was one goose shy of a gaggle and one brick shy of a full load.

Having the nerve of Dick Tracy, plus my positive attitude, has opened up many doors for me throughout my lifetime. From early childhood and into adulthood, the thrill of a new exciting experience and stepping out of that box that some call "normal" was what I looked forward to every day of my fun-filled life.

We lived in Mobile until I was fourteen. Then we said good-bye to our beautiful new custom-built brick city home. My sisters and I were looking forward to becoming country girls living on a farm. We left the city of Mobile and moved into our country home that we fondly named "Tara." The beautiful old farmhouse was furnished with lots of antiques and fine furniture that Mama and Papa bought to match the period of the house. The house also came with a hundred acres located in a small community not far from Loxley, Alabama, called Rosinton. Our farmhouse was 110 years old when my parents bought it in 1963 from an older couple who were from Birmingham, Alabama. The farm was too big for them to maintain any longer, so they sold it to Mama and Papa, who promptly began to renovate it. The house used to be a stagecoach stop on the original Spanish Trail. The locals named it "the old Banning place."

My sisters and I had our very own bedrooms upstairs with our very own balcony that overlooked the rolling hills. Huge oak trees with moss hanging from the branches lined our long driveway. It looked like an old Southern home you would see on a postcard or in the movies. I still remember the wonderful natural smells of the farm. We even had our very own horse, cows, and chickens with a chicken house. The locals told us we also owned the biggest bull in Baldwin County. The huge bull also had a French name, and he had huge balls that almost hung to the ground. I couldn't help but stare at them every chance I got. We also had a quaint and cozy guest house where I gave many a slumber party for all my newfound country girlfriends—Bettie, Martha, Sue, Barbara, Diane, and Theresa, who to this day remain my best girlfriends.

My girlfriends were so much more mature than I was. They wore makeup and knew all about boys. Except for one of my girlfriends named Leverne; she and I had so much to learn from them. They all wore the latest, most up-to-date fashions and looked like models with their huge tits and hourglass figures. I, on the other hand, had just gotten out of Girl-Scouts, wore a very modest training bra, and made Mama roll my hair every Saturday night so that I could wear my hair in ringlets to church on Sunday morning. I wasn't allowed to wear makeup or shave my legs until I was sixteen. Since I was so tall and very thin, some of the boys would call me "Olive Oyl" just to piss me off at the new school I attended.

I fell in love with all of my new girlfriends and wanted them to teach me everything, especially everything I wasn't allowed to do when it came to makeup and boys! Moving to the country from Mobile, I thought that all country girls were supposed to look like Daisy Mae and go on hayrides on Saturday night. Instead, they looked like they were in the twelfth grade, and I looked like I was in the sixth grade, when in reality we were all in the same ninth-grade class and were all the same age, give or take a month or two.

The best slumber party I ever gave for all my girlfriends in our guest cottage on the farm was a slumber party that would change my life due to a girl named Sue Linda. She was a couple years older than me and my other girlfriends. At a very young age, Sue Linda looked and acted just like the famous actress Sophia Loren. She had the same eyes, same attitude, but most of all the same beautiful body, and she loved to show it off! All of us were mesmerized by her huge tits, small waist, and perfect olive skin—but most of all, by her not giving a damn about wearing clothes. She would walk around with panties on most of the time and not think anything of it. She was totally uninhibited, and of course, we all wanted to be just like Sue Linda.

She was our hero, especially when she began to strip to some good ol' rock and roll songs. We all just sat there watching her every move, hoping that maybe she could teach us some of those stripper moves. Oh! How that girl could dance ... and oh my God, how I said to myself, *When I grow up I hope to hell that some way, if I could only learn just half of what Sue Linda knows, I could have any man I wanted.*

Of course, in Linnie's World, from that moment on, I had made up my mind that I wanted to go to Vegas and be a topless Vegas showgirl. I had a dream that if Sue Linda could do it, then by God, Linnie Delmar could do it, too! Then I looked down at my pitiful little skinny body with no tits, no ass, and no perfect olive skin. No way could I take off my clothes in front of my girlfriends, much less strangers. It hit me like a ton of bricks, and I said, *Welcome to Linnie's real world down on the farm.*

It was on the farm that I also met the first love of my life and the only boyfriend I'd ever had. His name was Donnie. I was in the ninth grade and he was in the tenth grade. He was tall and thin, with a perfect tan, hard body, blond hair, and blue eyes. The first time I saw him, I told Mama, "That's the boy I'm going to marry." Donnie and a friend of his named Ellis were fishing in the huge pond on our property, and Papa invited them up to the house for a cold drink. The rest was history. When my blue eyes met his, it was like magic. A switch went off in my head that told me, *All I want to do is be with Donnie.* Nothing else mattered—the hell with being a showgirl in Vegas when I had visions of marring Donnie. Mama kept saying that this was just a high-school crush, but I knew in my heart it was the real thing from the very beginning.

"If I hear the name Donnie one more time, I'll just scream!" my mom exclaimed. One of my best girlfriends, Bettie, told me so many times that if Donnie and I didn't get married when we grew up, she and I needed to move away to San Francisco and become flight attendants, flying all over the world.

Bettie saw the "big picture" of how she wanted her life to be long before she actually lived it. She went for her life goal as soon as she got out of high school. She was so smart and ahead of her time, even back in the ninth grade. She still is today. I, on the other hand, had no plans for my future, other than getting out of high school and marring Donnie, the love of my life. I knew he would take care of me for the rest of my life, and we would live happily ever after. I was such a dreamer back then, believing in forever love. I was going to stick to my plan just like Bettie stuck to hers.

To this day, Bettie is still one of my best friends. She has traveled all over the world as a flight attendant since 1968. She loves her job as much as she loves her beautiful city of San Francisco, where she still lives.

Two other friends, Barbara and Theresa, married the loves of their lives right out of high school and have lived happily ever after, just as I intended to do, way back then, with Donnie.

From the time I met Donnie, I never had my mind on important things that mattered, like schoolwork or actually learning something in school. All I wanted was Donnie to like me as much as I liked him. It was going to be a challenge, because he was The Man—the most popular football, basketball, and baseball player at our high school.

When Donnie did start to notice me and like me, and when we looked into each others' eyes, it was like magic. It was chemistry of the best kind. How did I even know what chemistry was back then? All I knew was that I wanted to hurry up and bypass all of this stuff called school and start playing house with Donnie.

The best part was that in no time at all, Donnie was into me as much as I was into him. At first he couldn't get used to my loud, outgoing, full-of-fun, crazy personality. He was kind of shy and reserved, very soft-spoken—not at all like me. That should have been my first red flag and the first sign that it would never work, but back then we had no idea what a red flag was. I was only going by what my heart told me to do.

"You can be as loud as you want and as outgoing and crazy," Donnie told me the first time we kissed. "Just let me kiss you anytime I want to."

For many years after he told me that, we were considered the perfect couple. Everyone loved Linnie and Donnie, and we loved all of our friends. From the very beginning, I knew Donnie was The One. He was the man I wanted to spend the rest of my life with. We would grow old together. In my sweet young innocent mind, back in the ninth grade, the path for the rest of my life was already set in stone.

Every chance Donnie had, he would come over to our farm, and we would do all the fun things that teenagers like to do, like ride horses, go fishing, go swimming in our pond, and just have lots of fun being young and in love.

Donnie's dad owned a working farm in Loxley. Donnie, being the oldest of five kids, worked very hard most all the time on his dad's farm, plus football practice. Donnie was a very busy fifteen-year-old, but I was just glad he had time for me in his busy schedule.

When my parents took me over to visit him, our parents would visit as well. They became great friends with each other.

It seemed like Donnie was always on the tractor plowing the field, and he would let me ride the tractor with him occasionally. I loved every moment of watching him plow, because all he wore was cut-off short shorts, no shirt, and high-top boots with white socks. Admiring his beautiful tan skin glowing in the hot sun would put my stomach in knots.

At the age of sixteen, I had my first orgasm just by looking at his beautiful hard body and kissing him. It scared the hell out of me, because I felt guilty that I had just experienced something that felt too good to me. Donnie and I were sitting on the sofa at his house and were only kissing when it happened. His mom came in and wanted me to hear some new songs she learned on the piano.

The worst part was, she wanted me to sit on the piano bench with her—I guess to cool me off and get me away from Donnie. Anyway, when I sat on the piano bench, I felt like I would be there forever and could never get up again. I ruined her seat on the piano bench and her sofa. I didn't have a dry thread on me from my waist down. It seemed like I was there forever. I could give a shit about the songs she kept playing that went on and on until finally the phone rang and she left. Donnie had no clue about what just happened because I never told a soul, not even my girlfriends. I was so embarrassed and mortified after that whole ordeal. I did let Donnie still kiss me, though, anytime he wanted to. Little did I realize then that I was already getting spoiled, looking at eye candy and not being able to take my eyes off the sight of a good-looking, half-naked man. This would get me in trouble as the years went on.

After only two years of living on the farm, in late 1965 my mama and papa sold it right out from under me and my two sisters without saying a word to us first or asking us if we wanted to move away.

Our world as we knew it was over, and we would have to say good-bye to all the wonderful friends we had made—and most of all, I would have to say good-bye to my boyfriend, Donnie. My sisters and I were in shock to say the least. Why would they want to ever move away from the best home we had ever owned and leave Tara?

It was all about making money—and with all the money they made, they had a chance to buy five acres in downtown Fort Walton Beach, Florida, on Racetrack Road, wherever the hell that was. They wanted to develop a mobile-home park for seniors, of all things. At age sixteen, I had never even been to Florida except once on a vacation to go see my granny who lived in Naples.

When we drove away from the farm, we all cried as we said good-bye to the best home we had ever owned. Mama and Papa cried all the way to the bank. When we moved to Fort Walton Beach, we moved into a brand-new custom-built four-bedroom brick home that was located on a beautiful large body of crystal-blue water. To make us feel better, Mama and Papa said that we could have our own ski boat parked in our boathouse at our back door and as long as we did our homework first, we could water ski anytime we wanted to. All *I* wanted to do was be with my boyfriend, and that's all I thought about. Since I knew he was The One, I couldn't stand the thought of losing him. So what if we had our own ski boat? All I wanted was Donnie!

I was not only sick from having to leave Donnie and all my girlfriends, but I had to start all over again making new friends at my new high school in Fort Walton Beach. I was in the eleventh grade and hated every moment I was there. At my old high school, I was so popular and active in every sport, and I was in every club. I was even going to try out for cheerleader just so Donnie and I could ride the football bus together after every football game.

Val hated it too because for the first time, we weren't in the same school together. Just in my eleventh grade class there were over five hundred kids, and I was totally lost most of the time, literally. I was depressed and cried a lot because I missed Donnie, and I just knew he might meet someone else.

To my complete surprise, Donnie borrowed his dad's black Ford pickup truck and came to visit me every other weekend. He said that he couldn't let me go either, because we were meant to be with each other. For the first time in my life, I heard those three little words I hungered to hear: "I love you"! I was seventeen years old. It was like a dream come true for me, and I began to be my happy little self again as I looked forward to seeing that black Ford pickup truck pull into our driveway every other weekend when Donnie came to visit.

The last part of my senior year, we found out that Papa had lung cancer and had only six months to live. We were in total shock and horror to hear that devastating news! On that same day, Mama stopped smoking and has never smoked since. They immediately sold our brand-new home on the water, and we had to move back to Mobile so that Papa could be near the best cancer doctor they knew, who was in Mobile. It was right after our home sold and before we moved to Mobile that Donnie came down for my senior prom and we had the whole house to ourselves, and believe it or not, Papa and Mama trusted me enough to let us stay in the house alone. We'd had lots of fun attending his junior prom and senior prom. Here was my chance to have the best time ever, prom or no prom! We went to my senior prom that night, and we slept in separate bedrooms when we got back home after the prom. I had made a promise to Mama and Papa that if they would allow Donnie to come down and take me to the prom, I would be a good girl and do the right thing. The thought of having sex did cross my mind at least a time or two, though. I had never broken a promise to my parents, and I knew this was a promise that was going to be hard to keep, but I did because I have always been a person to keep my word.

The next morning, we were supposed to drive back to Mobile to join my parents, who had left the day before. All we had ever done was make out, and of course, back then it was with all of our clothes on every time. Papa and Mama had done a very good job, so far, in bringing me up as a proper young lady and a good Southern Christian girl.

That morning, to my shock and surprise, Donnie wanted me to take a shower with him before we drove back to Mobile. Given the prime opportunity, of course, he took it! I was always so confident and bold, but that morning I turned into a quiet and shy flower who was not ready to bloom yet. I convinced myself it was only taking a shower, and it's not like we were going to have sex. I made sure the shower curtain was completely closed with him inside before I took off all my clothes. I was excited to finally get to see what that huge bulge looked like that he had kept hidden in his tight-fitting jeans after all these years! When we met, I was only fourteen, and now at seventeen, I had never seen a naked man. I was ready to see what the big deal was all about. I took one last deep breath and told myself, *I'm going in!*

I slowly stepped into the shower trying not to look at anything except his white teeth and, of course, those blue eyes. When I finally looked down and saw that huge thing with hot water dripping off the end of it, I was totally shocked! I jumped out of the shower so fast I pulled the shower curtain down on both of us and ran out of the bathroom to get dressed in my room, privately! I totally left him standing there dripping wet, big bulge and all standing right out there ready and willing. He was wondering what in the hell just happened when I screamed out, running as fast as I could to my bedroom.

I had no idea I would react to seeing that huge thing as I did, and neither did he. He was so embarrassed about the whole thing that we never talked about it again. In my sick, sordid mind, though, that's what probably started the pattern off for me having a huge appreciation for a well-endowed man. I love to look at a man's beautiful hard tan body, but then, what woman doesn't? When a real woman says that size doesn't matter, she's lying! All my girlfriends have the same appreciation for looking at a big handsome man, especially if they saw a naked man like Donnie.

I was only a child then, at age seventeen, and was so not ready to go there yet, nor was that flower ready to bloom, not for a while anyway.

We went back to being teenagers, and before Papa got sick, I was able to teach Donnie how to drive a boat, water ski, pull in a shrimp net, and do so many other fun things kids love to do when living on the water. After seeing what he had to teach me, he had his work cut out for him. But he knew it would be so much fun learning together as a couple, truly in love, wanting to spend the rest of our lives together. My senior year went by fast, because he kept telling me that he loved me, and we would always be together, and I believed him with all my heart.

Papa was so sick, dying with lung cancer. Instead of him passing away in six months, he lived a lot longer, with so much pain and suffering. He stood so strong in his faith that we all just knew maybe one day he would be well again and all our prayers would be answered. My sisters and I had never heard of lung cancer, much less known someone who had died from it. My sister Kim was now ten and her father, our papa, was dying and there was nothing we could do but pray for him to somehow get well and come back to us.

It was hard for me to understand how he could die when he read the Bible almost every day and was one of the most kind and loving men God had ever put on this earth. Having him to raise us as his own children was the best gift God had given us, so how could He take Papa away from us? I was so mad at God for a while for allowing this to happen to our loving family. Other than Mama and my granny in Ohio, he was the person I truly admired the most. He was the glue that held our family together, and I couldn't imagine our life without him. I especially couldn't imagine mama going on with her life without him. What would she do with three children living at home and her with no job? I prayed that if Donnie could be as good a husband to me as Papa had been to Mama, I would be a blessed and happy woman.

Chapter 2

HUSBAND #1—DONNIE, MY FIRST LOVE

Papa spent a very long time going in and out of the hospital in Mobile. During this time, the courtship between Donnie and me continued.

"Will you marry me, become my wife?" Donnie asked on a moonlit night, March 27, 1967, down on one knee in the courtyard of the hospital. Papa was once again in the hospital, and we had gone there to visit him.

Again, he shocked me, but this time he had all of his clothes on and held out a beautiful diamond ring.

"I picked it out myself," he explained. "I picked it out just for you."

"Yes, I will marry you," I answered, sealing the yes with a kiss that lasted several minutes. After dating him from my freshman to senior year of high school, I could not wait to say yes, yes, and yes!

We were married on July 27, 1967, at our beautiful Southern home in Mobile, because Papa was determined to walk me down the aisle. He was too weak and frail to attend a ceremony at our local Methodist church, so we had it at our home. That was fine with me. He was so sick and dying of cancer. I was just glad to have him there to give me away, small wedding at home or not.

It was the happiest day of my life and Donnie's, too. We were so great together and so much in love. The best part of it all, though, was that he could move out of his parents' house, I could move out of my parents' house, and finally we could be alone together.

We got as far as Pensacola, Florida, on our honeymoon and stayed at the first motel we came to. It was small, something like a Best Western.

Neither of us had any clue what we were doing. Finally, we were allowed to do whatever we wanted to do whenever we wanted to do it! Having that freedom was the best wedding gift of all.

Back then, our parents never told us one thing about sex, especially my mama, who told me more than once that the red bag hanging in her shower was for a bad headache.

I thank God that I can honestly say I was a virgin on my honeymoon. Now all I wanted to do was take a good look at what Donnie had wanted me to see for years and take my sweet time doing it!

Donnie had the most beautiful hard-toned body because he had been an athlete his entire life. As we got into making love, it took maybe five minutes tops for him to say we did it. It happened so fast we kept doing it over and over again just for the fun of it. We both felt so free to do whatever we wanted to do, anytime we wanted to do it. Life was good! I could tell from our very first night together that we would be doing this every night from then on.

We had our parents' blessings, and they wished us well. They were also ready to get us out of their house. They told us we were on our own now that we were a married couple. We had God's blessing to be as one, husband and wife forever.

Donnie also told me that a good Southern Christian wife was supposed to please her husband by having sex every night and twice a night on weekends for good measure. Again, I believed every word that came out of his mouth, even if he did pull that one right out of the sky! I did everything he told me to do and loved it!

Although our life was just beginning, Papa finally lost his long battle with cancer. He passed away the December after our wedding. We all were so lost without him. Mama had to start her life all over again as a single parent. My two sisters were still living at home.

About a year after I got married, Val married the love of her life, David—her own high-school sweetheart. They are still happily married to this day, over forty years later. They are still in love and very happy together.

Val has always been the smart one who went strictly by the rules and by the book. I always looked up to her as my role model. She always wanted to do the right thing and be the best wife she could be to David. She and David have always had that chemistry with each other that has held their marriage together like glue. They both knew that they had met The One from the first day they met and fell in love with each other in high school.

Val lets David kiss her anytime he wants to, just like Donnie had told me. I have always respected both of them and love David as the brother I never had. I always wanted to be just like my sister Val. She and David have held solid as a rock through the good times and the bad, especially when they lost their only son, Kirk. He was only twenty years old when he died in 1991 in a car accident.

Val is another person in my life who is good through and through—always has been and always will be. I am so proud to call her my sister. She has been the one person in my life who always made me feel smart and nothing like the blue baby I didn't want to be. In actuality, I never was that to anyone but Mama. In my heart, I also know that Mama does think I'm smart … I think. She just likes to keep me on my toes and mess with my head because I'm the oldest, and she thinks I'm the toughest.

My baby sister, Kim, was only ten when Papa died. Papa was only fifty years old when he lost his battle with lung cancer. She still misses the love and affection he gave her from the time she was born. I was also guilty of spoiling Kim rotten just like he did in her younger days and Mama to this day still does. After all, she's the baby of our small family.

Kim looks just like Papa, and she has his talent of playing music and singing and making furniture and other things out of wood. She is also an artist. I tell her all the time, "If I had only one ounce of your God-given talent, I would be out in Hollywood."

Kim's nothing like Val or me. She is so laid back, like Papa was, and never gets in a hurry. People compare Val and me to a buzz saw, never slowing down, always on the move, doing something all the time.

21

I will call Kim "Baby Sister" until the day I die, and I love her with all my heart. We remind her of how good Papa was to her and to us, and tell her all the time what a wonderful man he was and what a wonderful life he gave us up until the day he died.

When married life finally kicked in for me and Donnie, we were ready in every way to have the best marriage and the best life we could. We started out renting a small house in Rosinton about a mile from our old farmhouse, Tara. The small rental house sat in the middle of a forty-acre soybean field, and we paid seventy-five dollars per month for it. An older lady named Mrs. Marie owned the cute cottage and told us every month she felt guilty for taking our hard-earned rent money because we had fixed it up so cute and I kept it so clean, but she took the money anyway.

After we were settled into our home, Donnie got me a job as a teller at the local bank. He was at the local barbershop getting his hair cut, and the president of the bank was in the next barber chair getting his hair cut too. When Donnie asked him if he would hire me, he said, "Donnie, you were the best football player I have ever seen play. Tell your wife to start work on Monday." Donnie told me when he got home that I was going to be a teller at the local bank. I started work on Monday. I was more surprised by the fact that I started work on Monday than by the fact that Donnie got me my first job ever instead of letting me pick out what I wanted to do and where I wanted to work.

Donnie was in sales, working in Loxley, and he never really liked his job as much as I started to like mine. I knew one day he would find another job a lot better than the one he had, because he was so smart. Not even a year later, Donnie did find a job in Mobile that fit him better, and he loved it—although he had to drive to Mobile every day.

After settling into our daily routine for a couple years of married life, I talked about wanting to have a baby. Donnie had a plan about that, and we were going to stick to it. We wanted to start trying in 1969 because by the time he or she graduated from high school, the year would be 1988—and since 88 was Donnie's football, basketball, and baseball number in high school, it would be perfect for our child to graduate in 1988. How's that for having a plan? Again, it was Donnie's idea, and I loved it.

We spent almost every weekend in the summer at my mom's beach house in Gulf Shores. She had built a beautiful cottage on the gulf, and we loved having fun in the sun every weekend. Donnie had a passion for bass fishing.

For years, I had the habit of taking a moonlight swim in the nude every night before bedtime to relax me, but I stopped doing that after the movie *Jaws* came out and scared the holy Jesus out of everybody.

I didn't plan for it to happen as fast as it did, but on July 21, 1969, the day after Neil Armstrong became the first man to walk on the moon, our son was conceived. We didn't plan for it to be such a historic event, but just like Forrest Gump, I happened to be in the right place at the right time in history!

During an easy pregnancy, after my girlfriends gave me a huge baby shower, Donnie decided that he might pamper me for a change. He told me, however, not to get used to it. I was surprised and shocked that he wanted to do most of the cooking and cleaning in order to give me a break the week before our child arrived.

With a super-clean house to come home to thanks to Donnie, we were ready to welcome our son into the world. On March 27, 1970, exactly three years to the day after Donnie proposed marriage to me, Rodney was born. He looked identical to Donnie. It turned out to be the second happiest day of our lives. I was twenty-one years old, and Donnie was twenty-two.

We named our son Rodney after the famous actor Ryan O'Neal, who played Rodney Harrington on my favorite television show, *Peyton Place*. Martha, one of my best friends from high school, and I never missed an episode. Even when we were in the ninth grade, she would drive her dad's huge old Buick, which we fondly named "Big Bertha," over to our farmhouse, or I would ride my bike to her house, which wasn't far away. So Rodney was the perfect name, and Donnie loved it too.

Our healthy baby boy weighed seven pounds and six ounces and was twenty-one inches long. Not only me but everyone who saw Rodney said that he was Donnie made over.

We wanted to be the best parents we could be and raise our new son the best way we knew how. I went back to work right after Rodney was born. It was hard at times, trying to be a good mother, a working woman, and good wife to Donnie, but I felt like I could do it all. It was at times like this that my OCD came in handy for a change. I continued doing all the cooking and cleaning, making sure I still made love every night to Donnie. I was tired at times but looked forward to whatever time we could spend together. It's a good thing that I loved sex as much as Donnie did and always looked forward to bedtime.

Donnie was so smart, and he caught on fast and was such a good worker at his job in Mobile. His company noticed what a good worker he was and began the process of moving him up the corporate ladder. When his salary increased, we left our rental home in Rosinton and moved to Fairhope. We bought a brand-new 12x65 top-of-the-line Holiday mobile home. Back then we called them trailers. With our new baby boy and our new trailer, we thought we were living high off the hog! My mom had bought fifteen acres on Highway 98 in Fairhope and followed Papa's dream to develop it into a trailer park for senior citizens. When my mom began to develop the park, Donnie and I, to earn extra money, poured every cement slab and installed every awning on each trailer site on the weekends. Although it was a mobile-home park for senior citizens, Mama did allow a few couples to move in who were young in order to keep us company and so Rodney would have someone else to play with other than my baby sister, Kim. Those were some of the happiest days of our young married life, and I will cherish them forever.

Rodney had his first experience of playing in the snow on one of the few days that southern Alabama even had enough snow to cover the ground. Donnie and I got out playing in it like we were kids again, throwing snowballs at each other and playing with Rodney. Even though we were working hard but still not making a lot of money, we were so happy in love with each other and loved our son, Rodney. Our life was right on track, and so far, married life was perfect for both of us since we were still making love every day and twice on the weekends for good measure. That rule was Donnie's number-one rule of the entire household, and God forbid we ever break his number-one rule!

By the time Rodney was four years old, we had moved away from Fairhope to Pensacola for Donnie's job. He was made manager of his company's Pensacola office. He was one of the company's youngest managers and had moved up the corporate ladder faster than any employee they had ever hired. I was so proud of him. He was my hero!

It was a far cry from the small town of Fairhope, but whatever Donnie wanted to do was fine with me as long as we were together. Donnie told me that he would always be there to take care of me and Rodney, and I believed him. I didn't mind the fact that we were starting over, finding a new job for me and a new preschool for Rodney. My small income was always considered just fun money for extra groceries anyway. All I had ever done since I was eighteen years old was work as a bank teller.

It was not long before I was working again full-time at a local bank. It was located close to our new home. Believe it or not, I got that job on my own, without Donnie's help.

We enrolled Rodney in the best private Christian school we could afford, and he loved it. Every day he would come home very excited because he had learned another Bible verse that he had already memorized and could quote to us word for word. We were so proud of him and his progress of learning. We saw how smart he was on a daily basis. The school also had an after-school program for the working parents who couldn't pick their kids up until after five, which was perfect for our busy schedule.

We had moved up in the world. Now, instead of a 12x65 trailer, we had a beautiful brand-new three-bedroom brick home, a new bass boat, a new pickup truck for me, and a company car for Donnie. Life seemed like it couldn't get any better.

Although I was working full-time again and trying to be the perfect mom for Rodney, the perfect lover, wife, and best friend to Donnie, I still made time to have sex every night because I thought that's what every good Southern wife did. Donnie continued to tell me that, in case I forgot.

Each evening when he got home from work, I had a five-course meal on the table, including dessert. Of course, all my housework and cooking was done after I picked Rodney up from school and worked my eight hours, five days a week. Since I had very little rest during the week, I tried to get all my deep cleaning done on the weekends. I didn't want Donnie to have to do anything when he got home from work but get his rest, go bass fishing, relax, and of course make love to me.

Not once did I ever feel like he was supposed to help me do anything when it came to the household duties—I thought every wife in the world was doing just what I was doing, and like me, loving every minute of it.

Of course, my OCD was another thing that made me feel like I had to do it all and do it right then. Even if Donnie had wanted to help me out, I wouldn't have let him because I thought it was the woman's job when it came to doing anything in the household, especially doing all the cooking and cleaning.

This was my wonderful life, and my future goal was to one day get to work part-time instead of full-time. I wanted to spend more time trying to be a better mom for Rodney and continue to be the perfect wife for Donnie. Was I a stupid fool back then or what? Now I blame it on my OCD or just being brainwashed by Donnie's big dick! All I know is, even after all the love that kept me going for almost ten years, Donnie started acting somewhat distant toward me. I had no clue at first that anything was wrong because we were still making love every night.

In Linnie's World, how could anything be wrong when I was trying so hard to be the perfect wife, lover, friend, and mother to his only child? To sweeten the pot, I really thought every wife watched every football game on the weekends, although I hated football. Then it was our quality time together waxing his beloved new bass boat, which was the second love of his life! I think Mama might have been right when this blue baby even loved doing that for her man! When I think back on it now, how in the hell did I have all this energy to do all that I did? It had to be the sex and that big thing that was looking me eye-to-eye; every time I turned around, there it was!

All I know is, even after all the love and respect we had for each other during our almost eleven years of marriage, he began to act differently toward me, and I couldn't figure out why. As time went by and Rodney was almost six years old, life began to change for me and Donnie. He wouldn't come home until late some nights, and even on the weekends he would tell me that his district manager was in town from Houston, and they had meetings to attend and company business to take care of. Of course, I believed him—up until now, he had never lied to me, and we had never lied to each other. We always had total trust and respect for each other.

I even thought that since the times were changing—this was in the late seventies—I might even think about cutting my long auburn "Cher" hair off shorter. I was ready to change with the times and roll with the flow.

It was all about women's rights, free love, Woodstock, and rock and roll! Donnie wouldn't hear of me cutting my hair. He loved my long, straight, dark auburn hair, small waist, and big boobs. I always stayed a size eight up until this present time, when I turned sixty and then went up to a size twelve, which is still where I am to this day. I still have the huge boobs, but not so small a waist. In Linnie's World, I keep thinking that my tiny waistline might show up again one day and surprise me. I even think that on some days, I see a glimmer of it in the mirror and believe in my silly mind that I'm still that perfect size eight and can wear all my favorite sexy clothes. Thanks to Sue Linda, the sexy clothes and pole dancing were the thing to do for my man. Any time he felt sexy and wanted a show, he got one. Thanks to her being at that slumber party when I was fourteen years old, she changed my life and Donnie's, and he loved it. When Donnie kept coming home later and later back then, I began to wonder if I was still sexy or pretty to him or not anymore.

Since his district manager kept coming to Pensacola more and more often, Donnie was putting his work and his job before me and Rodney, and we saw less and less of him as time went on. I tried not to be angry with Donnie for putting this distance between us and this wall up that he seemed to be hiding behind, but nothing was working to get through to him. In the late seventies, there was no such thing as marriage counseling. I felt like he was completely shutting me out of his life, and it was like a sharp knife had been taken to my broken heart; we had always been so connected and so close to each other.

I was living my worst fear of losing him, and it was a nightmare to think of my life without him. I made the worst mistake in our married life by telling my mom that we were having some problems. She has always been my best friend, and I needed someone to talk to. The first thing she said to me was that he had to be cheating with another woman. I assured her that wasn't it, and he was just a workaholic spending too much time at the office putting his job first and us second.

Back in the late seventies, when a man cheated even once, the first thing people would tell you to do was to go get a divorce, because if he cheated once he would do it again. Back then, I failed to see the pattern Mama always had, which was to escape when things got rough and hard to cope with. Her pattern was always to not look back on the past and learn from your mistakes. Maybe she was like that because she never married her first love or her high-school sweetheart like my sister Val and I did. We had the good luck to marry and stay happy with the love of our lives, and she didn't. If I only knew what I know now, I would have paid attention to my mom's advice and listened to her words of wisdom and experience.

For the next few months, the tension was not only thick at home between me and Donnie but at work as well. My boss and her husband were having problems in their marriage just as Donnie and I were, if not worse.

Every time my boss's handsome husband, who looked just like Clint Black, would come in to visit her, he would make it a point to talk to me too. I didn't realize at the time that she had been telling her husband all about the problems Donnie and I were having. I had to tell her what the problem was when I kept coming to work and crying for no apparent reason.

Her husband, from day one, always told me how pretty I was and what pretty blue eyes I had. This was music to my ears. Of course, not a word was ever spoken when his wife was around. At that time in my stressed-out life I felt anything but pretty, because I had lost weight. Barely over a hundred and five pounds did not look so good on my five-foot-eight frame. I was skin and bones, and I stayed depressed all the time. I couldn't get over the reality that Donnie and I had grown apart after all these years of having such a good marriage.

Donnie's schedule of having sex every night went on as usual, but now my heart wasn't in it, and I was feeling more and more alone. Like a normal loving wife, I didn't want just sex, I truly wanted to feel wanted and needed and, most of all, loved now more than ever. I would cry at odd moments, with no warning or control of my tears at all. My perfect world would never be the same again, and poor little Rodney had no clue what had happened to his mama and daddy.

By now, things at work were heating up between me and the Clint Black look-alike, my boss's husband. The more I tried to pull away from him, the more and more he would want to talk to me and act like he and my boss were worried about me. He was saying all the right things for a silver-tongued devil. According to him, they had been talking about a divorce, and it had been over a year since they'd had sex. He told me that probably within six months, they would be divorced.

My boss never told me about any divorce. She always said they had a lot of problems they needed to work out. I sure didn't want to get on that list of problems. I needed this job now more than ever, because I didn't know what the future had in store for me and Rodney.

As time went on, and Donnie was pulling away from me more and more, I was thinking Clint Black was looking better and better to me. God help from me for thinking that, but that was all I could think about because it had been months since Donnie really looked at me or talked to me as his wife and best friend. Plus the sex was few and far between now, so I knew we were in trouble.

I was now more confused than ever. I had lived a lifetime of always doing the right thing, living a good Christian life with my husband and my son. I was supposed to be on the straight and narrow as a mother, a good wife, and a good homemaker, and taking so much pride in myself, in my son, in my husband, and in our home. For years I was always happy, content with my life and with our life as a married couple and as a family.

I began to think that maybe my OCD had something to do with our marriage not being on the right track. I spent more time trying to be this perfect person and perfect wife to Donnie—and no one is perfect, especially me. I believe I was more in love with the idea of having a perfect marriage than with Donnie himself. I didn't know how to connect with Rodney because I never put his wants and needs first—I was too busy putting Donnie first, and my child always came second. I had no idea who I was as a person and not just Donnie's wife. Through the years, I had lost my true sense of myself as an individual. I was more concerned with the idea of how our relationship looked to others than with the relationship itself. I was more in love with the idea of being the perfect mother to Rodney than in doing something about it on a daily basis.

Ladies, always remember to never let a man come before your child's wants and needs and time spent together. I made that mistake, and although Rodney turned out to be a well-adjusted and responsible adult, I never knew how to relax and enjoy him as I should have. I can't remember one time taking quality time with Rodney when he was five or six years old by taking him to play at a park. Any park would have made Rodney happy. Donnie and I both were guilty of never playing with our only child and taking time out of our busy schedule to do simple fun things with him like pushing him on his swing set in our own backyard. I was too busy putting my husband's needs first, and my child's needs came second. I missed out on the most important years of his young life, and I will never get them back. To this day, I still regret being so blinded by my own wants, needs, and desires and not Rodney's. Don't ever make the same mistake I did.

A couple of weeks went by. I was letting the silver-tongued devil nip at my heart and soul because I was so hungry for an emotional connection with someone, nothing more and nothing less. I was beginning to have thoughts of doing this unforgivable deed of screwing my boss's husband. It was on my mind a lot, and the Clint Black look-alike was hot on my tail every time his wife wasn't looking. I had gone over the line of not only thinking about it but wanting it to happen. I wanted someone who just wanted me and someone who made me feel loved again. Donnie had taken all that away from me, and I was looking to try to get it back somehow, some way, with someone who just happened to be the wrong man. He only wanted me because he couldn't have me. Plus, he was married to my boss.

By now, I was more confused than ever, and his silver tongue was looking better and better all the time. Looking like Clint Black sure did sweeten the pot. He was about six foot two and a hundred and seventy-five pounds, with no fat on him anywhere. He wasn't the man I wanted, though. I wanted my husband to love me again like he used to.

I just wanted my husband back any way I could get him! I had this crazy idea that if I told Donnie there was a good-looking man after me, I could make him jealous. He would forget work and wake up and smell the coffee, appreciate what he had, and realize he might lose me to another man. He would break down that wall of being distant to me, and our life would be on the right track again. I felt like I was a piece of clay that Donnie wanted to make into a fine piece of art, when all I would ever be to him was a piece of clay he could mold into a pot to cook in, and without that pot he could never eat again. That analogy says it all about how raw my emotions were and how I was feeling.

My mind was so messed up, and the sad part was that God was no longer driving the bus that was about to go off the cliff of no return—I was! I was lost already in God's eyes; all the praying in the world wasn't working, so I stopped praying. God had left my heart and soul, and I felt like I was only a shell of a human being who no longer had a heart or soul left in me. Words can't begin to describe how lost and lonely I felt at that time in my life.

When my boss finally told me that she and her husband were getting a divorce and she had already seen an attorney, it was like she had given me the green light to go through with my plan of making Donnie jealous. I told her that Donnie and I were also walking on thin ice, but we had not yet talked about a divorce. For some reason, her telling me that made what I was about to do seem to be all right, but still my heart and good common sense told me otherwise.

After work one evening when Donnie was picking up Rodney from school, I told him that I had to stay late at work for a banking class that I had to attend. The silver-tongued devil was in his brand-new pickup truck, and I was following him in my pickup truck. He wanted us to go to a motel. As soon as he mentioned that idea, I screamed out that I could never go to a motel because that would make me feel too dirty! He told me to follow him because he knew a place to go in the woods where he used to deer hunt. Since it was close to my house, I said what the hell and followed him deep into the woods—as if that were any better than a motel. After we arrived deep in the woods, God only knows where, he picked me up like a five-pound bag of sugar with no effort at all. For a moment I felt like a princess when he carried me from my pickup truck to his truck; my feet never touched the ground. He gently sat me on the back of his tailgate on his brand new bed liner. All of a sudden it hit me like a ton of bricks, and I had an epiphany. In my loud outside voice that I'm sure woke up all the forest animals and probably some wayward deer hunters, I screamed out, "Oh my God, this is wrong, I can't do this. How do I get out of these woods?" I knew at that moment how much I loved my husband, and I could never do this to him.

A few seconds later, I was saying how sorry I was to let this happen and for it to go this far. I got the hell out of those woods as fast as I could go. After I calmed down from the worst panic attack I have ever had, I couldn't wait to get home to my family. Donnie was the only man I had ever been with, and I knew at that moment I didn't ever want to be with any man other than him.

The guilt I felt was overwhelming for days until I couldn't hold it back any longer. I made the biggest mistake of my life up to that point. I should have taken that secret to my grave and never told a soul about that day deep in the woods. Instead of cheating on my husband to make him jealous, all I did was have a panic attack in front of a redneck. The Clint Black look-alike turned out to be a jackass when I told him good-bye and to never speak to me again! I told Donnie what had happened. For the first time in his life, he was shocked and numb to the point where he couldn't talk. He slowly walked over and got the only suitcase we owned from under our bed and began to pack it with all his clothes. He told me in his soft gentle voice that he was leaving me, and he wanted a divorce. If I had only known then what I found out later about all of his secrets that I'm sure he would have taken to his grave, I would have helped him pack and not been so hard on myself, throwing myself under the bus every chance I got.

I was in a panic that he was really leaving me and Rodney and was never coming back. I began to beg him to please stay so we could talk, and he told me he couldn't stand the fact that I had been with another man, much less my boss's husband. I told him that nothing happened, and the reason I let it go that far was to make him jealous. It was at that point I knew all the talking in the world wouldn't help. He didn't believe a word I was saying. I had broken that circle of trust, and no words could bring back what we had lost.

Donnie left us that night, and I have never since felt so alone and so lost in God's eyes. I felt at that moment that everything leading up to this point was my fault, and I was for certain going to hell for what I had done. Now what was I going to do to try to get him back? I hated myself so much—not because I went into the woods with my boss's husband, but because I was so stupid as to tell Donnie something that I should have taken to my grave, because nothing happened. What happened was that I realized how much I loved my husband! I couldn't even look at myself in the mirror. When I did look, all I saw was a reflection of a lost soul and a bad woman. I had gone against all my morals and principles just to try to get my husband to love me again and come back to me. My plan to make him jealous came back to bite me in the ass and telling him about it was, to this day, the biggest mistake I have ever made other than moving forward with a quick divorce.

For over a week he was gone, and Rodney and I had no clue where he was or where he was living. I went to his office several times in the hope that he would talk to me and forgive me, but he had nothing to say to me. I was so physically sick after what I almost did to my boss, I quit my job the next day and never saw her again. I wasn't eating at all and crying all the time. I was five foot eight and weighed less than a hundred pounds. I looked like walking death to say the least.

Donnie could have gone a lifetime and never known my secret, but my big mouth had to 'fess up and be honest, thinking all along I was doing the right thing by telling him. That was the first of many biggest mistakes of my life, and I had to live with what I had done. I had to face the fact that my life with Donnie was over, and the love of my life was gone forever.

When Donnie and I finally talked, he told me all the things he knew would kill me. Physically, it almost did. Mentally, I kept telling my pitiful self that my marriage could in no way be over because I was, after all, the perfect wife, lover, homemaker, and mother to our son, Rodney. I just knew somehow he would come back to us and truly believed it in my heart and soul. Of course, that day never came, and I ended up leaving my beautiful new home, all my new furniture, the new bass boat that I waxed every Sunday for him.

I did everything that a good wife was told to do and like a pure fool, I enjoyed the hell out of it. All I took when I left to move back home to Fairhope was my son and my pickup truck, plus some pictures of our almost eleven years together as a family. I was done, and I didn't want any material things that reminded me of the ten good years of marriage we did have. I wanted to start over fresh but had no clue of how to do that since up until now, Donnie had told me what to do and ruled my life, not just because I let him, but most of all because I loved him.

He had been my whole life since I was fourteen, for God's sake, and I felt totally lost without him. The divorce happened so fast as far as the legal paperwork went because I was so upset I had no more fight left in me. I had no will to live any longer if it had not been for my beautiful six-year-old son. He was the only reason I had for getting out of bed every day. The day that I signed the papers at the attorney's office, my best friend Pat went with me for support, and as we left the attorney's office that afternoon, she looked at me and said, "Let's go to Happy Hour, you look like you need a drink."

I said, "What is Happy Hour, anyway?"

Pat knew I wasn't a drinker, but since she too was going through her own divorce, she thought it would do us both some good. She knew since I couldn't stop crying that a drink might calm me down.

In the back of my broken heart, I knew I had just made the biggest mistake I would ever make in my life. The reason for our divorce was in black and white written on our divorce papers that said it all: "Our marriage was irretrievably broken" were the exact words, and so was my heart.

I was a single woman now with my whole life ahead of me. It wasn't until years later that the feeling of loss would finally be fulfilled with joy and contentment for the person I have become today. At this point, I couldn't imagine what was in store for me. I had no idea that my future would be full of traveling all over the world, meeting interesting people, even A-list actors, and owning my own business one day. Then, I was at rock bottom, and each day was a struggle to even get out of bed much less care for my son who needed me so badly. I couldn't seem to pull myself together.

When Rodney and I moved back to Fairhope, we moved into a 12x60 furnished rental trailer that belonged to Mama. It was the same trailer park in which Donnie and I had poured every patio slab and put up trailer awnings to make extra money when we were so poor but so happy. I felt at home, though, because Mama and Kim were only a few trailers down from me and Rodney. I went back to work for the local bank where I had worked years ago and got my old job back as a teller. They were so glad to have me back, and I was so glad to just have a job again. My only income now was my tiny little paycheck from the bank and the $175 per month Donnie gave me for child support. Donnie has always been a good dad to Rodney. He would get Rodney every other weekend so that they could spend some quality time together and maybe take time to finally know each other and have some fun together as father and son.

Years later, Donnie ended up marrying a really nice girl much younger than him and, believe it or not, she had a six-year-old little boy. Donnie ended up raising and being a good stepdad to him. Rodney was six years old when his dad left us for another life, and now Donnie had married someone who had a six-year-old son in his new life. I still wished Rodney had a full-time dad when he needed him the most, and I missed having a husband.

So I couldn't help but be bitter over the fact that Donnie was being a full-time dad to new wife's son instead of our son. It wasn't long before that feeling went away, because she was a good person and has always been very nice to me. She was a very good stepmom to Rodney, and he loved her from the very first day he met her. I'm so glad that Rodney has an extended family that will love him unconditionally. They care as much as I do about his well-being and have his best interest at heart as I do.

Rodney did graduate from Fairhope High School in 1988, just like Donnie and I had planned. After high school, Rodney got his degree from Auburn University in hotel and restaurant management. He went on to manage three restaurants at the Auburn conference center, working his way through college the whole time. After graduation, he took a job as a banquet manager at the Ritz-Carlton in Atlanta. He was in charge of huge banquets and parties for famous people such as Jimmy Carter, Jane Fonda, Al Gore, Elton John, and the list goes on and on. These days, Rodney is a very wealthy and successful real-estate salesperson in Atlanta and has been Salesperson of the Year for his company several years running.

Now that Rodney is a grown man, he and his dad are as close as ever, and even Donnie and I maintain a good relationship with each other. People always say, "You never forget your first love," and for us it is true in so many ways. My memories now of being married to Donnie are all good memories that I will cherish forever. I have forgotten the few bad memories so that we can be the best of friends for our son's sake and ours too. I will always love him, as he will always love me because we have a wonderful son together. We have known each other since I was fourteen and he was fifteen. We were only kids back then, and now both of us being in our sixties we have some cherished childhood memories together.

It was a wonderful ride from the time we were teenagers to this present day, growing up with each other. Of course, in Linnie's World, if I had it to do over again, I would have spent more time being engaged with our life instead of never slowing down to smell the roses. I don't blame it on my OCD, I blame it on me being more in love with the idea of marriage and how it should be instead of the marriage itself and rolling with the flow of life. It was the real deal for us, and we did have the chemistry that you only may find once in a lifetime or maybe twice if you're really lucky, like Donnie was when he found Rodney's stepmom.

I know enough about myself now in the present day to know that if I had stayed married to Donnie, I would have never discovered the real person I have become today. I am happy to know that I have discovered a side of me that was there all along, but I never knew it. I have an adventurous soul that loves to travel and step out of the box of what some people call normal. I love owning my own business and being a person who can help pamper stressed-out people each and every day. I was always meant to be an LMT, and going to Hollywood to work with the movie stars has been a bonus to the surprises my life has blessed me with and given to me.

It has taken years for me to realize that meeting that perfect soul mate we all want and living that fairy-tale life is just in the movies and not real in most cases. In my heart and soul, I'm so happy for Donnie and his wife and their two other children, because now Rodney has a sister and brother who truly love him a lot as their big brother. In Rodney's future, all I want is for him to be happy, and to this day I know he is.

Donnie too is happy, and along my path of life I have had many experiences where I have been happy and content as I am today. I take each day and make it the best day of my life. It's never a dull moment, and in Linnie's World, it never will be. I make every moment a moment of no regrets and keep that smile on my face and that happiness in my heart and pleasure in my soul.

Chapter 3

MOVING TO THE REDNECK RIVIERA

As I drove over the Intracoastal Canal Bridge onto Pleasure Island, the Redneck Riviera became the start of a new world for Rodney and me after my divorce from Donnie. I had a local contractor build me a small beach house on West Beach Boulevard. I proudly named our new home "Linnie's Summer Dream." After growing up on the water, it was like coming home again, and it felt good. I have always loved the smell of the salt water from the Gulf of Mexico, and the sound of the waves splashing on the beach was music to my ears. It was the fresh new beginning I needed to start my life over again. I had a positive attitude that life on the beach was going to be the start of some new memories that Rodney and I could cherish together. Little did I realize that this was the beginning of an adventure that would change my life and turn my world as I had known it upside down!

I used the lot that Mama had given me for my down payment to secure the $27,000 loan to build my home (now lots are $150,000-plus across the street from the gulf), and of course I was able to get my employee's interest rate by working at the bank. That made my house payment a whopping $216 per month. My paycheck only averaged $120 a week before taxes and insurance were taken out. I'm still amazed how I managed to be a single mom with a seven-year-old son and no help from my mama at all back then. I was on my own. Now I realize what a blessing she gave me by not giving me anything and everything I wanted throughout my childhood. She did me a favor by letting me become a woman on my own at the age of twenty-nine, single and alone. She taught me the best lesson you can teach a child before they become an adult, and that was how to do a hard day's work and stand on your own two feet with no help at all from anyone but yourself. I had to grow up fast because I no longer had a husband to take care of me like I did before I moved to Gulf Shores.

Back in 1978, though, I still wondered how I was going to manage this large house payment on what I made as a teller at the bank where I still worked. Somehow each month we made it, and we loved our cute little house we had made into a cozy new home. It had two very small bedrooms and one bath with an open kitchen and living room. I even had my own fireplace and a big deck on the front and back of the house. It was up on pilings, so I had a carport, storage room, and laundry room under the house. I had one thing installed in that small little house that no one else had on Pleasure Island. It was two huge mirrors on the ceiling of my master bedroom, hoping one day soon I could see the new Linnie back in action again mentally, physically, and hopefully sexually as well. Sex had always been a huge part of my life, and I enjoyed the hell out of it. For God's sake, how could I not enjoy something so pleasurable that happened every day of my life for over ten years of marriage to Donnie? I went from every day to zero within a few months. What a change of lifestyle, and I was feeling it already with no man in sight.

Rodney and I moved into our beach house on August 16, 1978, exactly one year after Elvis died, and life has never been the same for either of us! This was a far cry from Pensacola, living with my husband, and a far cry from living in the small rental trailer at the trailer park in Fairhope. I was so thankful that my sweet Mama had given me the start I needed to begin my life again. She was there for me then, and to this day she is still there for me now when I need her the most. I still love and cherish the time we spend together each and every day.

When we moved to the gulf, Rodney was in second grade at Foley Elementary School, and from that day until the tenth grade he hated every moment of it. He told me he just didn't fit in with all the local good ol' boys, and he felt so out of place. I could never understand why he hated it so much. He still managed to make good grades throughout his school years and was really active in the high-school marching band once he got into the seventh grade.

Rodney had made friends with a boy named Patrick, and I became instant best friends with his mom, Lynn. She was the manager of one of the local motels on the beach in what is now known as Orange Beach. Her motel was named the White Caps Motel. She and Patrick lived there, above the office. She was the first of a lot of new best friends I went on to meet and with whom I still keep in touch to this day. Some of my other best friends were Rhoda, Pat, Myrtle, Marcie, Sam and Shine, Rick, Melissa and Hamp, and my special little buddy, Wanda. Her nickname went on to be "Wild Wonderfully Wicked Wanda" because she dated Kenny Stabler for many years. Rodney and I were a second family to her famous little dog, Omar, which Kenny had given her as a make-up gift. It was the best gift he had ever given her during the eight years of dating the famous football star. We would keep Omar when she and Kenny would travel during his last few years with the Oakland Raiders. To this day, she and I are still the best of friends. Now she keeps my little dog, Coco, when I travel around the country with friends on my Harley-Davidson motorcycle.

I really became a woman when I moved to Gulf Shores. I was getting used to being all alone; trying to raise my son the best way I knew how, on my own for the first time, still felt so strange to me. The first thing I did as a full-time resident of Gulf Shores was join the Gulf Shores United Methodist Church. I was trying my best to get back on track by letting God take the wheel and drive the bus again. I tried hard to get back in God's good graces and do all that I could to be a good Christian lady again.

After working for years as a teller at the local bank, I was ready to try something new. I ask the locals to keep their eyes open for me. All the locals welcomed me and Rodney with open arms and kind words of support that I was so hungry to hear. Gulf Shores in 1978 only had 2,100 permanent residents. I took my time looking for a better-paying job and a job I enjoyed doing. I was sick of counting everyone else's money. I needed a job that fit me better than just being a teller at the bank. I knew with God's help the job would find me.

While still working at the bank, I reignited a longtime friendship with a local contractor I had met years before when I was only eighteen years old and working at the local bank in my hometown where I grew up. Now he was a very successful businessman, very soft-spoken, dressed well, the nicest person you would ever want to meet, and he had the most beautiful blue eyes I had ever seen. They were as blue as my eyes, and he always made an effort to talk to me and tell me how pretty I was every time he saw me. He had all the right moves and said all the right things that I wanted to hear.

Yet he, too, was a silver-tongued devil. I loved every minute of his slick ways. His name was Al, and from one look at him I knew he was trouble with a capital T. For years, he was my favorite customer. He only wanted me to wait on him when he came into the bank. Now here he was living in Gulf Shores, and here I was living in Gulf Shores too. Little did I know that this one man was about to turn my dull, lonesome life upside down and rock my world!

One night my mom, who had still not remarried since Papa died, and some of her lady friends invited me to go out with them to some local nightspots such as the Gulf Gate Lodge and the Blue Jay Lounge (which was later named Nolan's). I said, "Why not?" I was single now, and Rodney was with his dad in Mobile for the weekend. This would be my first time out on the town with the girls. I was looking good and feeling better about myself, especially now that I had gained a little weight in all the right places. It was pretty late by the time we arrived at the Blue Jay Lounge. When the band started playing the song "(Lying Here with) Linda on My Mind"—which happened to be my favorite song—out of the darkness a good-looking man came slowly walking over to our table. All the ladies, including me, couldn't stop staring at him. He held out his hand and, in a soft sexy voice, said, "Linnie, come dance with me." Lo and behold, it was my dear friend Al! I had only seen him behind the counter at the bank and thought then he looked good, but that night I took a good look and saw a whole new sexy side to him. At that moment, he already had me at "hello"!

As he took my hand to dance, it was like magic not only for me but for him, too. From that moment on, I had no idea how much my innocent young life was about to change. I couldn't believe my very first time out on the town with the girls—or as my dad would say, "right out of the chute"—I would fall into the arms of the man of my dreams. He and I had a different kind of chemistry, like no other. I had never felt such passion as we felt for each other every time we were together. That night we ended up dancing the night away, like so many more nights for almost eight years. I felt so alive when I was with him, and the excitement was like a raging fire burning inside of me. He was the only man I wanted in my life because I felt safe with him. Maybe it was because he was married. When we were together, he made me feel like I was the only girl in the world he wanted to be with and make love to.

I didn't like being involved with a married man. I knew it was wrong, especially in God's eyes, but in my blue eyes it felt so right. The desire to have lots of sex, have fun dancing, and drink too much far overpowered the right thing to do at that time in my life. I let the man, with his good looks and smooth ways, play me like a fool—but a very happy fool. He had sparked a fire in me that I thought had gone out forever, until I saw what was between his skinny little legs that even put big Donnie to shame. I couldn't get enough of him, nor him of me. Even if I couldn't have had sex with him, I would have paid my last dime to just look at what he carried around in his pocket all the time.

His huge attitude had my attention, and I didn't even look at another man for years. I became known as Al's number-one girlfriend. Little did I realize until years later how many other women also had their attention on what was in that deep pocket of his. He was very famous around Baldwin County, especially on the Redneck Riviera. He seemed to have everything I was looking for in my next husband. He had charm, he was nice, he had those beautiful blue eyes, and he was rich. Best of all, he had what every one of his girlfriends wanted, and that was just to have one night with him to see what the real prize was. That chance is what we all hungered for and couldn't get enough of.

Every night we spent together, I felt like I had just won the lottery. He acted like he loved being with me as much as I adored being with him. So far, though, he and Donnie were the only men I had been with. Back then, all I could think of was how could I be so blessed and so lucky to have the man of my dreams (although he was married and totally unavailable), a new beach home, and a healthy son who loved me no matter what I did. I was in hog heaven and having the time of my life. I loved every moment of it, and there was never a dull moment living on the Redneck Riviera.

Now all I needed was for Al to get a divorce so that we could get married and live happily ever after. Of course, this entire reality coming true was, in Linnie's World, lots of fun, lots of sex, and total happiness. I dare not forget Rodney getting a new stepdad and me having the perfect husband of my dreams who was rich … and had a big dick too, as a bonus.

As the years passed, things did not go at all according to the plan I had envisioned and dreamed of. My life again wasn't on the right track, and again I wasn't allowing God to drive the bus. There were times that my happy, wild, perverted lifestyle of so much sex and fun felt like I was in a fog. I was going through the motions of everyday life and doing what was necessary to take care of Rodney, but that wasn't fair to Rodney or me. Again I felt like a failure and didn't know how to engage and be a better mother to my only child. I was letting sex take over my life. I was desperately searching for that happy Linnie who loved married life.

I wasn't happy with myself as a person, much less happy with the person I had allowed my love for Al to turn me into. I didn't blame Al, I blamed myself for letting the sex take over my life; that's all I could think of. I wanted to be that good Christian Southern lady again, and not the party girl I had turned into. All I wanted was to be a good wife and take care of my son and my husband like I used to do when I was married to Donnie. I missed being that good person and that lady who I wanted to be again.

If I had married Al and he had a bass boat, I would have made the time to wax it for him, like I used to do for Donnie, and enjoy the hell out of it. I really thought in my sweet, kind heart of hearts that the day was coming soon, and I would welcome and embrace it with open arms. Of course, all these dreams and ideas of that perfect life would not come true for me anytime soon. Again, I was more in love with the idea of marriage than I was in love with Al himself, and again I wanted to be living the fairy tale of happily ever after with the man of my dreams—or so I thought.

At times, when new men or tourists would come to visit Pleasure Island and want to talk to me or date me, Al's friends would stop them in their tracks. Men quickly knew to stay away from me because I was Al's girlfriend. Many times Al's friends like Billy, Hamp, Kenny Stabler, Joe Gilcrest, and Robert would watch over me when Al wasn't around. They made sure I was taken care of until Al arrived to really take care of me as a boyfriend should do. They were my bodyguards, friends, and protectors. It did make me feel special, because his other girlfriends weren't treated as nicely as I was treated by the locals. After all, Al was the kingpin of Pleasure Island and everyone knew it. Everyone also knew about our affair. At first I felt really bad that I was dating a married man, but after the first night with him that bad feeling went south. In my heart, I knew his wife had to know because she was a smart person with a lot of class. Actually, she was a very nice person. Gulf Shores was a very small town, and everyone knew all about your business and made it a point to find out if they didn't know. In later years, I took on a newfound respect for his wife due to what we all put her through, especially me and Al. She had her man and she, to this day, has stood by him to the end. She wound up being the smart one out of all of us, and if this is my chance to say I am sorry, well, I am sorry more than you will ever know. He is so very lucky to have such a good woman who truly loves him—not just because of what's between his legs, but what was in his heart the whole time: You, my dear! All of us who had our fun times with Al just wanted what she still has—a loving husband who can look into her eyes and say, "You are the one" and really mean it.

The time I was spending with Al took my mind off of Donnie and the wonderful ten-plus years we spent together as a married couple. The years with Al seemed to fly by because we were having such good times with each other and with all of our friends. To this day, I still don't want to give up on my dream of maybe someday finding that one man who will tell me, "Linnie, you're the one!" He's out there somewhere, and with God's help he will find me and we will find each other. *For God's sake, where is he?* That was the question I kept asking myself in those days. I still had not found out who the real Linnie was. I had no idea what to do about it because I was still allowing the sex to take over my body and my life. I was still just a shallow shell of the woman I had turned myself into. I blamed no one but myself for letting this happen to me.

After years of wanting things to change between me and Al and getting tired of being Al's party girlfriend, I noticed a tall, slim, good-looking man who kept showing up in Gulf Shores. He would always stay at the White Caps Motel where my friend Lynn was the manager. She kept saying she wanted us to meet because Rodney and Patrick, her son, really liked him, and they hit it off good together. His name was Merle, and he was from Tallahassee, Florida. She and I named him "Merle the Pearl," and he was nice … but my heart wasn't looking for anyone else but Al. The day came when Merle and I finally did meet. Merle made me look at him and ask myself, *What I was doing waiting on a man who I could never have?* Merle knew all about my relationship with Al because Lynn told him. He told me that he wanted us to get to know each other and that I should take as long as I needed to get to know him as a good friend. For Rodney's sake, I took a good look at him, and we ended up going out several times on an actual real date when he was working and staying in the area. He had a good job selling private mortgage insurance to the bank where I worked, of all places. He said that Al's friends had already told him to stay away from me—but he liked a challenge, so Al's friends didn't scare him. I knew then he was on a mission to slowly work his way into our life and win me over. The hard job was, how would he be able to get into my cold heart that was frozen with doubt about finding someone other than Al to fall in love with? He was right, I had no desire to warm up to him because I truly loved Al, or thought I did at the time.

After months of him wanting us to be more than friends, I gained respect for him for not giving up on me, and started letting him into my world little by little. He and Rodney had become the best of buddies, and I saw how much Rodney needed a father figure in his life more than just every other weekend with his dad, Donnie.

Lynn and I became the den mothers for eight little Cub Scouts with Merle's help and guidance. Merle also gave me the money to buy school clothes for Rodney. He would build and fix stuff around my house and also Lynn's house and the motel. He was falling in love with me, but for some reason, I never liked him as much as my friend Lynn did. There was something about him, though, that I did like—he loved to spend money and time on me and Rodney. The sky was the limit, and I was certainly not used to that.

Al never bought me anything but all the drinks I wanted when we were out on the town with our friends. Everyone probably thought he made my house payments or bought me my little orange MGB sports car because his wife ended up having one just like mine at the same time. But he never bought me one thing or paid any of my bills. I always paid my own way, and it felt nice that Merle the Pearl wanted to spend some money on Rodney and me. Merle even bought Rodney a brand new go-cart so that he and Patrick could ride it on the beach. I didn't realize it at the time, but he was using Rodney to get to me, and it was working. For the first time in a long time, I could see that Rodney was really happy, and that made me happy. Rodney had a man and a real friend who wanted to do things with him and for him. Little did I know then that Merle the Pearl wanted to be a good stepdad to Rodney and more than just a good friend to me.

The way I saw Gulf Shores was far different from what the tourists, new business owners, and developers saw on the outside looking in. It was my home. It was a big sandbox of fun, sex, and no rules or boundaries for the locals. We took full advantage of all the freedom, lots of sex, drinking, and late-night dancing at the Gulf Gate Lodge, the Blue Jay Lounge (Nolan's), the Pink Pony Pub, and the famous Flora-Bama. The owner of the Flora-Bama, Joe Gilchrist, made us feel like VIPs each and every time we walked through the door. He still does make us feel special when we see him nowadays. He's a local who has been there every day and seen it all through the years. He's a good person and a loyal friend to all of us who had the pleasure of being regulars at the most famous bar/roadhouse of all times, the Flora-Bama. If we wanted to stay out really late, Al and I and all of our friends would go to the Keg. We finished the night off with a game of pool before going home to make love. That was the place to see and be seen on late nights.

On Thursdays, all the banks would close a half a day and all the popular people like me, Rhoda, Melissa, and Kim would go out on Robert's famous shrimp boat, the *Thelma Ann*, for which I was the number-one deckhand. I kept the boat clean and spotless after every fishing trip because my OCD would kick in. We would tie up near Ono Island with Kenny Stabler's boat he named the *Honky Tonk*. We would go deep-sea fishing in the crystal-blue waters of the gulf. We would bring the shrimp nets in with jumbo shrimp, all of which were cooked on the back deck of the *Thelma Ann*. We would share our catch of the day, our silver queen corn, and Baldwin County new potatoes with famous football players, movie stars, and coaches. They would drink hundred-dollar bottles of wine with us until they were knee-walking drunk and passed out. The wine and booze never ran out.

When it got too hot on deck, we would ride the shrimp ropes that pulled the shrimp nets and not see any danger in any of the crazy wild things we did back then. We all had beautiful, buff, tan bodies with abs of steel, and we knew we were hot and sexy! Many times we thought nothing of diving off the twenty-foot fly bridge of a million dollar yacht to show off in the crystal-blue water of the Gulf of Mexico near Alabama Point. We had this true paradise all to ourselves, and we loved it. Not many people knew of our beautiful sugar-white sandy beaches at that point of time. We would have kept it that way forever if we could—but the secret was getting out more and more each day of what a perfect paradise we lived in on the Redneck Riviera. The locals ruled, and we had more fun in one day than most people have in a lifetime. I was so lucky to be there at that time when I was young enough to enjoy every minute of every day we all spent together as one big happy family on Pleasure Island. I was living the good life and was hoping things on the Redneck Riviera would always be the same. Little did I realize how things would change after a hurricane named Frederick hit our beautiful Gulf Coast on September 12, 1979.

The fall and winter was also fun for the locals because we had the whole beach to ourselves, and the island came alive after sunset. We could walk for miles down West Beach or East Beach and never see a soul, especially at night when we wanted to make love on the beach cuddled up behind a sand dune or go for a moonlight swim in the nude. Some of the locals would be so drunk from Happy Hour lasting until midnight. Many times me or Rhoda would drive them home and dump them off in their front yards as their wives would yell out the front door, "Thank you for getting him home safely!" There was no way we were letting these men drive themselves home. Since I was Al's girlfriend, I knew everyone, husbands and wives too. From judges to city councilmen to the mayor, we all were having a good ol' time and living life to the fullest on our very own Pleasure Island, the Redneck Riviera. Those times will always be cherished and remembered by those who lived them every day and more so every night. I was a den mother to all their children in the daytime in the real world. I was Al's girlfriend and soon-to-be wife in Linnie's World.

I hungered to be more available for Rodney and a better mom for him when he needed me the most. He was always my reason to keep on wanting us to have a better life. I wanted to end my wild ways and wilder nights as Al's party girlfriend. I was looking at Merle the Pearl to help settle me down, if that was possible. He knew he had his work cut out from day one. I think he saw me as a challenge, and he was right.

I had never been with another man but Donnie since the ninth grade and had never drank or set foot in a nightclub until after our divorce. I had turned out to be buck wild after moving to the Redneck Riviera and Pleasure Island and meeting Al. I was enjoying being single and not having to answer to anyone other than my son. I wasn't sure if I wanted to be tied down to just one man other than Al. I still loved and felt safe with Al as my friend and lover. Time would tell if Merle the Pearl would fit into my wild life in Gulf Shores and my wild friends who were like family to me and to Rodney.

I still loved the fact that, when Rodney was with his dad every other weekend, I wouldn't think anything about getting in my fancy little sports car with the top down and taking off with one of my girlfriends on a short trip of a day or two. We would sometimes drive south down the beautiful Gulf Coast into Florida.

A trip that I will always remember was when I took off one weekend with Pat, who was the manager of the bank in Gulf Shores. We went to see the Daytona 500. We had no tickets and no place to stay in Daytona, but that didn't stop us. Off we went on one of Linnie's many wild adventures and another Forrest Gump moment of being in the right place at the right time.

We pulled into the Holiday Inn that was right across the street from the Daytona 500 racetrack. I went into the hotel to see if we could, by chance and with my good luck, get a room for the next two days. Lo and behold, at the moment I walked in someone had just canceled, and we got a real nice room for the next two days. Knowing how hard it was and how expensive it was to get tickets for the race the next day, I told Pat to look across the street at the racetrack. I told her to put on her best walking shoes, because we were going to climb over that really high fence close to the racetrack. I explained to her that after we get over the fence, we would be able to climb to the top to the highest hill (which turned out to be on the top of the tallest embankment of one of the sharpest curves on the racetrack) and watch the race from that viewing point. Best of all, we wouldn't even have to buy a ticket and could watch the race for free.

As conservative as Pat was, breaking the rules by climbing a fence where we weren't supposed to be was completely out of the question. I told her to trust me, and let's start walking. To my complete surprise, she did. As we got closer and closer to the fence that I wanted us to climb over, the higher and higher that fence was looking. All of a sudden, while we were walking, a brand-new yellow Cadillac with two good-looking men pulled up beside us and asked us where we were going.

Without batting an eye, still focused on the fence, in a firm positive voice I said, "Do you see that high fence over there next to the racetrack? We are going to climb over it so that we can actually see the race on top of that huge hill because we can't afford a ticket."

As they looked at me in shock—probably thinking, *What in the hell did she just say?*—one of them said in a very sexy soft voice, "Ladies, hop in, we have a better idea."

As trusting as I have always been, I told Pat to get in the car first. She turned around and gave me that look of doubt that I had seen before and said in her soft, calm, sweet voice, "We don't know these guys, much less us getting in the car with them. Do you really think that's a good idea?"

Pat was one of my best friends. She was born with a birth defect that for some reason had turned her butt into a huge bubble butt, something like you would see in a porn magazine. I also told her that if God played this dirty trick on her by giving her this so-called huge bubble butt, that if she could have only given me just one half of one cheek it would make me the happiest girl in the world. This would make her laugh every time. I told her that I had a good feeling about this and about these two guys so get your big fat ass in the car right now, and she did. It was a two-door sporty new Cadillac. I was behind her, and I was pushing that big bubble butt into the backseat as hard as I could! I suddenly realized we were going in the wrong direction past the entrance to the racetrack where everyone else was going. I ask them where were we going, and why did we pass the regular entrance? We were going in the wrong direction. They said that we were going through a tunnel and then into a place fondly named "Pit Row." They ask us if we brought our camera, and I told them it was around Pat's neck. They said that we might want to take a few pictures of some of the more famous race-car fans. Tom Cruise, Paul Newman, Robert Duval, and some other race-car fans would be down in Pit Row. Then they handed us two gold VIP passes. They said to keep them around our necks at all times, and we promised we would.

After the look of shock and surprise left Pat's face and mine too, it was like we had gone to race-car heaven. It was my first time to go to a car race, much less a Daytona 500, and Pat's too! We planned to take pictures all day and stay as long as we could thanks to our two new buddies we had just met less than an hour ago. It was like a dream come true if you like watching fast cars and good-looking men. "Pit Row" had it all. Before the men let us out of the car that day, I asked them how they got a hold of these passes. They said that one of them owned one of the famous race cars and the other was a race-car driver. They said that during the time trials (whatever the hell that meant), the car was wrecked and they were out of the race, but that wasn't stopping them from being there and watching the race that day. With a big smile on both of their good-looking faces, they said good-bye and to enjoy the race! We thanked them and they took off into the crowd of thousands of people. We never saw them again.

Pat looked at me with a big smile on her face and said that she would never doubt me again when I said that I had a good feeling about something, and she never did. We both have never been back to a car race since that memorable day at the Daytona 500. A day to remember in Linnie's World of never a dull moment, and a Forrest Gump moment of being in the right place at the right time!

Chapter 4

HUSBAND #2—MERLE THE PEARL

I continued to date Merle for a few months, and finally I made up my mind that Rodney needed a new stepdad and I needed someone to help me get away from Al and make me an honest woman. On June 6, 1981, I married Merle the Pearl, and although I never liked him as a friend, I was hoping that with time I would grow to not only like him but maybe love him too. I felt that Rodney needed him a lot more than I did. Merle had spent a lot of time with Rodney, and I felt like he really loved my son. Rodney, on the other hand, liked Merle a lot but never loved any man other than his dad, Donnie. Merle didn't have any children or any baggage that I knew about from his past, and he wanted to be the best stepdad he could possibly be to my only child.

From the very beginning, something told me that Merle wasn't all he seemed to be. He had a lot of good things that I liked about him, but when he drank he had a dark side that I felt very uncomfortable with. Up until the day we married, I had only seen that dark side twice, which wasn't a pretty sight. I should have known after one time that it was a red flag not to continue this relationship, but he convinced me he would stop drinking. One of my best friends, Rick, who was an usher at the wedding, told me I

51

didn't have to go through with this wedding. He saw the fear on my face and told me it wasn't too late to tell everyone to go back home, the wedding was off. I wish now I had listened to him and gone with my gut feeling, because it told me, *Don't do it!* I went through with it anyway. Rodney walked me down the aisle at the Gulf Shores United Methodist Church that day. The man standing there to meet me for the rest of my life was drunk as a skunk! Merle the Pearl looked at me with glazed-over cold eyes as if he was as much in pain and fear as I was, but I was sober. I couldn't believe that he was drunk on our wedding day. I couldn't believe that I was going to settle for a man I wasn't in love with. Everything inside my entire body was screaming out, *Help me God, what do I do now*? God was right there all along showing me the biggest sign I needed to see—Merle standing there drunk as a skunk—but I failed to open my eyes and see the sign He gave me. I failed to listen to that loud voice or that gut feeling telling me to stop the wedding and tell everyone to go home. I was more afraid that Mama would kill me because it would be so embarrassing to our whole family than hearing what God was trying to tell me all along. I felt like I was at the point of no return, and I was about to make a huge mistake when I said, "I do." What I should have said was, "Run, Linnie, run, as fast as you can!"

Trying to be the sweet Southern Christian girl who was getting my life back on track again, I walked down that red carpet and said, "I do." I knew it was a huge mistake as soon as the words came out of my mouth, and like a fool I went through with it anyway. Rodney was eleven years old, and I loved him more than anything in the whole world. I had always hoped and prayed that his stepdad would be Al, but that again was only in Linnie's World of hopes and dreams that would never come true. All I could do now was hope and pray that Merle the Pearl wouldn't pass out on the floor of the church while we were exchanging our vows and maybe die right then and there on the spot.

After the wedding, everyone went back to my home on West Beach, where we had a small reception for family and friends on a huge deck that Merle had built on the back side of my house. The new addition was going to be a room where he could put his furniture. He also said that he was going to pay for the remodeling with his bonus check from his job. The addition was as big as my beach house, and the expense was mounting, but he said for me not to worry because it was taken care of. I was fool enough to believe him and trusted that he wasn't going to screw up my cute little beach house that Rodney and I had made into a charming home. During our reception, he began to drink even more. I was praying that he wouldn't fall off the deck, which was fifteen or twenty feet high off the ground. It had no hand railings around it. If anyone fell off the deck, especially Merle, he could be hurt or killed.

Thank God my new husband did not fall, but he did go skinny dipping later that evening with some of his wild friends from Pensacola who I had just met for the first time. Rodney, Mama, and I were cleaning up along with one of my best friends, Pat, after everyone had left our so-called wedding reception. They said that they would never forget this wedding because it was like a train wreck they couldn't stop watching. The people from Pensacola saw Merle naked in the gulf before I saw him naked on our wedding night, which I spent alone in my bed while he slept it off on the living-room sofa. Thank God Mama had taken Rodney back home to Fairhope with her and my wonderful new stepdad, Steve. The next day, Merle woke up just like nothing had ever happened the night before, and although it didn't happen in the bedroom, he said he didn't remember anything after he said, "I do." I kept telling myself, *Linnie, what in the hell have you gotten yourself into marrying this drunk who you don't even like, much less love?* For the next couple of weeks, Merle tried to make it up to Rodney and me. I could not forget his behavior in front of my family and friends and especially in front of Rodney, who he kept saying he loved so much. Rodney had seen how he acted and lost some respect for him, just as I had.

From the first day we got married, Merle wanted me to quit my job and travel with him on the road. His district for selling private mortgage insurance to savings and loans included Alabama, Georgia, and Florida. He knew I would say no because Rodney was in school and couldn't be left alone. The following summer, as soon as Rodney got out of school, I finally did quit my job at the bank so that Rodney and I could travel with Merle. He took us to wonderful places throughout the Southeast. We stayed at the best resort hotels, and he spent lots of money on both of us like it was nothing because he was trying to make up for all of his mistakes.

Merle wasn't drinking as much—at least I thought he wasn't, because he would hide it. We had not been married a month when on July 4, 1981, something happened that changed everything. We had gone to Point Clear where my stepdad, Steve—who loved me and my two sisters like his own daughters—and Mama owned a huge beautiful home on Mobile Bay. It had a nice boathouse on the end of the pier where we would have cookouts and do a lot of boating when we weren't in the huge hot tub on the screen porch facing the bay. Since it was July 4, Merle bought over two hundred dollars' worth of fireworks against my better judgment. I let it go because I was trying to get along with him; he was drinking heavily that day. That night, he was on the deck playing with Rodney and Kirk, who was Val and David's son. All of a sudden, I heard Mama screaming. The wind had blown one of Merle's lit firecrackers right on the top of Mama's head, and her hair was on fire! I thanked God that I was sitting next to her, because I was able to put the fire out with my hands before it burned a hole in her head and burned her hair completely off. I got so mad at him that I told him to get the hell out of there and never come back, because when he got to drinking he saw no danger whatsoever in his actions. To this day, I have never been so mad at any one person in my entire life. That same night, my mama had already forgiven him and wanted me to do the same, but I could not let it go. She has always had a forgiving heart and never liked conflict to be an issue. I've very rarely heard her raise her voice or argue with my stepdad to this day. She just holds her hand up and says, "Talk to the hand," which means to stop talking and let it go. Then she changes the subject.

Merle stayed gone a couple of days until finally, when he did show up at my house in Gulf Shores, he told me he was so sorry and asked if I could ever forgive him. I told him unless he went to rehab for his drinking problem, don't think for a moment that our marriage was ever going to last. He left for rehab the next day ... but only stayed there for a week before telling me he was cured of drinking, and now he knew he had to quit. Like a fool, I wanted to believe him, because I was not going to fail in this marriage as I had failed and bailed out so quickly with my first marriage to Donnie. My thoughts again were that I wanted Rodney to have a father figure in his life every day and not just on the weekends that

Donnie had him. I wanted Rodney to have a stepdad who he could look up to and have respect for. When Merle wasn't drinking, he was so good to me and, most of all, good to Rodney; he couldn't do enough for us. He could fix anything or build anything to perfection and loved doing it. He also could cook and clean house as good as I could and loved doing that too, if it made me happy. When he was drinking, he turned into an entirely different person who was mean as a snake and a complete asshole in every way. Slowly, he was trying hard to earn back our respect for him the best way he knew how and doing the best he could do to improve himself.

One evening when Rodney was spending the weekend with his dad, Merle and I went out to eat, and since a new popular game had just come out, I wanted to play it. It was called Pacman, and everyone on TV was talking about it. The only place in Gulf Shores that had a Pacman machine was my favorite old hangout, Sam and Shines. Of course, I ran into some of my local buddies and close friends who were so glad to see me. Since I was a stay-at-home mom now and trying to be the perfect little wife and homemaker, I never went out at all unless I was with my husband.

That evening had been pretty calm and relaxing up until a good friend of mine named Butch said hello and asked how I had been doing. Butch was one of a few tough guys who looked like they had just escaped from prison; he was a big strong man with lots of muscles. He lived on Pleasure Island. A few years earlier, I had invited him to my housewarming party after Hurricane Frederick. He had never forgotten that invitation because he had never been invited to any big party, much less a private party inside someone's home, because of his bad-ass reputation of drinking so much he would want to fight and maybe really hurt someone or try to kill someone.

There was one story that the locals told about Butch that made everyone fear him, especially the cops. It was a Sunday night at the Flora-Bama. He had been drinking something other than beer when he was handcuffed to a Gulf Shores cop. He got so wild and crazy that by the time they set the cop free, Butch had slung him around like a rag doll. Butch almost killed that cop. The officer had to spend a week in the Foley hospital with a broken arm and broken hand, which he would never be able to use again. To say the least, when the cops were called again because bad boy Butch had been drinking too much, they stayed as far away as they could. I never knew if that story was true or not, but I thanked God that Butch always liked me. He went out of his way to be nice to me and whoever I might be with at the time.

All the locals loved Butch, and they had a special respect for his space. They also knew that, unless you were invited by Butch into his space, you didn't dare go near it or near him. This time I was with my husband, who was so jealous and insecure; words could not describe what an asshole he could be when he was drinking. I'm sure it's because he was an alcoholic— and a jealous mean one at that.

I was having so much fun playing the game Pacman that I didn't notice what Merle was up to. The next thing I knew, Butch, in a very calm way, was softly tapping me on the shoulder and saying to me in his calm inside voice, "Miss Linnie, I think I just killed your new husband."

When I went outside on the front porch of Sam and Shines to see what had happened, Merle was nowhere to be found. Some say he had told Butch something like, "Don't ever speak to my wife again, you smart-ass redneck." All it took was one punch to Merle's nose, and he was down and out for the count. Others say that after the hard blow to the face, Merle the Pearl slithered off the deck and under the deck like a snake that had just been run over by a Mack truck. All I knew was that, by the time he got home hours later, after getting a ride to the Foley hospital ER, he told me how foolish he felt. He should have listened to me when I warned him not to say anything, not even one word, to Butch or he just might kill you. He believed me now after Butch had broken his nose and fractured his jaw in two places.

The next time I ran into Butch, a few weeks later at our only local grocery store in Gulf Shores, he apologized to me again. He said that he had to hit my new husband because he was being such an asshole. I told him it was all right and not to worry because Merle had learned his lesson, to not be such a smart-ass, which he often was, even when he wasn't drinking. I also told Butch that when he was drinking real heavy he turned into a very jealous, mean, and insecure asshole and probably deserved exactly what he got.

Butch said something to me before he walked away that I will always remember, something priceless that made me respect him even more as a dear friend. He looked me in the eye and said, "Miss Linnie, if you ever need me to come down to your house on West Beach, just let me know. It will be the last time that asshole will ever be mean to you again." He quietly smiled and walked away. Guess what? Butch never said too much, but I knew he meant what he said, and he wouldn't think twice about taking care of that pain in the ass that I called my husband. The wicked thought of *Way to go, Butch* did enter my mind once or twice, I have to admit. Butch just became my hero and my new best friend.

It was a couple of months later when Rodney and I finally said that we couldn't take anymore. Merle had tried to convince us that six to eight beers a day was normal. We were tired of locking ourselves in my bedroom while hearing him break up the furniture, screaming and cussing in fits of anger. Thank God it was his furniture he was breaking up and not our furniture—or us! Too bad I didn't have a phone in my bedroom to make that phone call to my good buddy Butch. The next morning, Merle would have all his furniture put back together, as best he could. He would cook a breakfast fit for a queen and would act like nothing was wrong. He never remembered how mean he was to both of us. The whole time Rodney and I were locked in my bedroom, waiting for him to sober up, we were always in fear of what he might do to us when we did come out.

I was at the end of my rope and so was Rodney, so instead of calling Butch for that big favor he said he would do for me, after eighteen long months that really felt like eighteen years, it was over! I kicked Merle's alcoholic ass out and filed for divorce, and I have never looked back. I never saw him again, and neither did Rodney. Now that Rodney is a grown man, he says that every time he looks at a Budweiser beer can he thinks of our ordeal and what we went through with Merle the Pearl.

I told Rodney over and over again how sorry I was to have put him through that nightmare, and that my second marriage would probably be my last. Rodney and I had never been exposed to anyone who was an alcoholic and had no idea that anyone could act like that. It wasn't a pretty picture or one we ever wanted to see again.

Our home was a mess because the addition Merle had added on to my home was incomplete with lots of construction still to be done. Now, instead of the cute little beach house that was the perfect size for me and

Rodney, we had a huge duplex with an even bigger second mortgage on it. I could no longer afford my house.

My mom stepped in once again to come to my rescue and bail me out. She took over the second mortgage, and my dad finished doing the construction on the duplex so we could live in the front part of the house and my mom could rent out the back part. Rodney and I had a lot more room but missed our original little house we had made into a home together. The best part of our home now was that we weren't living under the same roof with an alcoholic asshole, and we had peace of mind. We both were safe when we went to sleep at night with only the smell of the salt air and the sound of the waves from the gulf as music to our ears.

As soon as I got my house in order, I had one big thing on my mind. I wanted to see Big Al again. When Rodney was spending the weekend with his dad, I went out on the hunt to find Al and hold him in my arms again after eighteen long months of not seeing him. I went to our favorite place, which of course was Sam and Shines. I wasn't there very long when Al walked in the door. After we danced to our theme song of "(Lying Here with) Linda on My Mind," we left to go back home and make love.

To my complete surprise, he had already heard the news of my divorce and acted like he couldn't be happier for me. Of course, I was hoping he also had good news for me that he was now single and his divorce was also final. This was only in my dreams, because he was still married and didn't want to talk about it. After all these years of us being together, I was still the other woman, and at that moment I embraced the thought of it. I never brought up the subject of him getting a divorce again. I was overwhelmed and happy to be holding him in my arms again. I felt safe for the first time in eighteen months. It was then that I told him I loved him for the first time and had missed him more than words could express.

To my shock and delight, for the first time ever, he told me that he loved me too, and he had always loved me but wasn't one to express his feelings. The year was 1983, and since 1978, all I had wanted to hear him say was, "I love you." My reaction was of course joy and excitement and visions of our future together as a couple. Instead, a week or so later, he had a pool party for me at one of the many condos he owned. All of our friends were there, and we had a ball for a while during the short time we were all sober, but after one bottle of wine, I was terribly sick to my stomach. All I could think about was that I had fallen back into the same old bad habit that I was trying to make a clean break from. I kept asking myself if I really wanted to have a life with a married man who I knew in my heart had always been in love with his wife instead of me?

Al didn't seem to mind at all when I left the party early to go home alone, because he'd also had too much to drink. Being the other woman wasn't at all what it was cracked up to be. So many times I was sick of being alone, hoping to see him out somewhere and hoping he wanted to be with me and not with one of his other girlfriends who had the same visions and dreams that I had of being Mrs. Al, if only for one day or, even better, one night with him. Getting to see that big beautiful thing between his legs drove us all to do things we couldn't help ourselves to do. We all wanted the big prize. Most of all, we wanted him, but we knew in our heart of hearts that there was only room for one lucky person in his heart, and that person was smarter than all of us—his tolerant, sweet wife!

I found a better-paying full-time job than what I'd had at the bank. During my spare time, I did some modeling to make extra money and feel like a local movie star. My girlfriends who modeled with me, Anna and Rhoda, were famous as well. I modeled swimsuits, business suits, Mardi Gras gowns, and fur coats all provided by Wesley Burger, who owned the most upscale boutique on Pleasure Island, named Burger's, which was located in Gulf Shores. I also did a lot of shows for Pendleton business wear out of Atlanta and New York. The fashion shows were held all year round, and some of them were even on television in the Mobile area and in Birmingham, such as the Tom York show. Many times the shows were held poolside at Holiday Inn and the Gulf State Park Convention Center or the Grand Hotel in Point Clear, which was the happening place to go see and to be seen on the Eastern Shore. Other popular places we had many fashion shows were Top of the Port, owned by my dear friend Eddie Spence and his brother Mike, and the Sportsman Marina, owned by none other than the kingpin himself, Big Al. Let's not forget the famous Gulf Gate Lodge that Sally and Joe McCarron owned. During Happy Hour, we had many shows to entertain not only all the locals but some tourists and new developers moving into the area to build condos along our beautiful slice of heaven. Times were changing for us on the Redneck Riviera, and I was ready to roll with the tide and explore some changes of my own.

One of my best friends, who happened to be gay, was my hairstylist Eddie, and he also did the hair and makeup for all of our fashion shows. Everyone loved Eddie and Howard, his longtime partner. Howard was the best and only interior decorator in Gulf Shores at that time. Everyone also loved Wesley Burger, who was the owner of Burger's Boutique. The three of them were the only gay, good-looking, successful businessmen living in Gulf Shores. The three of them were, of course, my best friends who kept telling me to hang in there with Big Al because they had as great an appreciation for a well-endowed beautiful man as I did, if not more. They understood my devotion to him, and like me, they just knew any day now his divorce would be final. To this day, I still have lots of gay friends, and they are drawn to me like a magnet for some reason. I guess because I am fun and carefree like they are. I'm also different like they are, and that sets us apart from anyone else. My whole life up to any point, good or bad, I have yet to see or want to see a man who wasn't well-endowed. Merle the Pearl was no exception. It was almost like looking at a freak show or looking at a train wreck that I didn't want to look at but I had to because it was there. Not only me but all my girlfriends, to my surprise, were also size queens—but their luck, they said, wasn't nearly as good as my good luck had been, so they were still searching for their perfect Donnie and Big Al to look at anytime they wanted to. Like me, they kept asking, "Where is he?"

Being a certified model with a modeling agency out of Pensacola for many years, I always stayed a size eight and could still eat anything I wanted to at that time in my life. I am five feet eight inches tall and one hundred and thirty pounds, with big blue eyes, a small waist, and big boobs. I always kept asking myself, *Why in the world wouldn't Al want to marry me?* I never thought once about maybe I wasn't the smartest goose in the gaggle, or maybe being that blue baby Mama thought I was had something to do with it. I tried to convince myself that I was as smart as my sisters or any of my friends by keeping a positive attitude—and most of all, keeping a great sense of humor to mask the pain I was in for not being the best mom I could be for Rodney. I still had many regrets over continuing my relationship with Al and wanting to be with him as often as I could.

When my friend Rick, the same friend who told me that I didn't have to marry Merle the Pearl, got me a full-time job as the head of customer service at the Gulf Shores Plantation, I really felt smart! Little did I realize then that my OCD and attention to detail were the real reasons he hired me. Rick knew I would be perfect for that job and do it better than anyone else could do with the help of my OCD.

I had a small one-bedroom office on the beach that faced the Gulf of Mexico, and I was in charge of making sure all 519 units had every piece of furniture and accessories in them down to the last coaster and pot holder. It was like I was on a mission trying to keep everything in its place and seeing to every last detail in all the units on a daily basis until all my owners took ownership.

I was the on-site representative for the developers, and I also worked closely with the rental management company when my new owners turned their units over to them to rent. I made sure the construction punch list was complete on all the units, working with the contractors. Most of all, though, I made sure that all of our owners were happy owners.

I loved this job and did so well with the 519 units that US Capital, the company I worked for, sent me to several of their twenty-three resort properties throughout the United States.

Macy, a girl I worked with, and I would travel to properties in Atlantic City, New Jersey; Silver Creek, Colorado; Hilton Head, South Carolina; and Myrtle Beach, South Carolina, where I had twelve hundred condos. We had a ball, working some days fourteen and sixteen hours, loving every minute of it. I met new people and worked with lots of new, good-looking contractors who loved Macy and I like sugar. I would wear my pink hard hat and my short shorts on my tanned body, and we would drive them crazy. But for some reason I never dated any of them; I kept it strictly business.

I made more money on just overtime each week than I made for a whole month at the bank. Life was getting much better for Rodney and me. I did have to travel all over the country with my job, but my mom and stepdad would pitch in and take care of Rodney for me when I needed them to.

In the summer when Rodney was out of school, the company would fly him to whatever part of the country I was in, and he would be our gofer all summer. He got to see big cities like I did, and we even took a trip to New York City one time for a long weekend when I was on a property in Atlantic City. It was one of our best trips together, along with going out to Hollywood when he was almost fifteen, where we rented a Rabbit convertible and he drove the whole time we were in Los Angeles.

I was even able to buy Rodney his first car at age fourteen. The Gulf Shores police knew that he was driving, but they asked me to black out his windows so that they couldn't see him actually behind the wheel; after all, that would have been breaking the law. Me being Al's number-one girlfriend, I had some perks. Al knew the mayor, city councilmen, and judges. God forgive me for going against their rules or breaking the law. I would bake cookies and make my famous fudge for the whole police department to thank them for their kindness and for keeping those blinders on just for me and for Rodney until he was sixteen. That was how close the people were on the Redneck Riviera and how friendly they were to each other.

Everyone knew everyone, and during the time that Hurricane Frederick hit us head on, we grew even closer helping each other through the hard times as well as the good times. We would pool all of our food together and eat big meals at the Gulf Shores and Orange Beach Community Centers with help from all the locals and the Red Cross. We were one big happy family, and when outsiders would even try to make their way into our family, it was not an easy task. To this day, the locals still rule Pleasure Island.

We also had an unspoken rule that we never would kiss and tell. All the married men, including lawyers, judges, and city officials who were in high-paying positions, knew they could trust some of their well-kept secrets with some of the local ladies who would take those secrets to the grave. Al knew he was safe with me because I would never say or do anything to hurt him in any way. We all knew that his loyal wife was aware of us—especially me—and any of his other girlfriends telling his wife was totally out of the question. We were all about him being able to come out to play every chance he got, and he liked to play as often as he could, whenever he could.

When it came down to the truth of it, we had been using him all those years as much as he had been using us. Sex, especially good sex, has a way of becoming our number-one enemy. It can be used against us when it comes down to a person's inner feelings and tarnishing their good reputation. It took many years and many heartbreaking moments for me to come to that realization. As we get older and wiser, they say that not enough sex is bad for our health and too much sex ... well, there is never such a thing as too much sex. That's what makes the world go round!

With my new job and me being out of town, Al began to play with the new lady in town. Her name was Mrs. Mancy Pill; she was married to some doctor in north Alabama, but she had a summer home on Ono Island. She was a lot older than me and Al, too, and she was very pretty. She had two things going for her that I didn't: she had lots of money to spend on Al and on real estate for Al, and she did not have his heart. His wife still had his heart, and I still had his most charming asset anytime I wanted it, which by now was few and far between. He was in high demand for all of her attention, and she made it known that if she was going to spend her husband's hard-earned money on Al, she did not want me or any of his other friends in her way. She wanted him all to herself!

One evening, I received a surprise visit from Mrs. Mancy Pill. To my delight and surprise, she knew all about me. She wanted to know all about the women who had been in Al's past. She asked me why I was the only one he did not deny having an affair with when she cornered him for an answer. I was nice to her because, after all, she had brought me not one but two bottles of the most expensive wine you could buy. I guess she thought if she got me drunk, I would tell her everything there was to know about how to please her new love interest and the kingpin of Pleasure Island. Little did she know that I'm not a big drinker, never have been and never will be; I can take it or leave it. Also, little did she know that I would never break the circle of trust that took years to build—and especially wouldn't give her the pleasure of telling on my lover of almost eight years, off and on.

Al was a hard nut to crack, and as good as the sex, lies, and fun were, I was not giving her a damn thing to make it easier for her to try to steal his heart when he had stolen my heart and innocence years ago. It was up to her to play her games of how to be the other woman in his wild, sordid life. She was going to have to learn the hard way, as I had, that no matter how much money she might have or how pretty she was, he wasn't going to leave his true love, his devoted wife. Mrs. Pill made it clear that she wanted me to stay as far away from him as I could, and I made it clear for her to get the hell out of my house and do not ever come back knocking on my door again. I had failed to tell her that as soon as possible, I was planning to move away to Fairhope, because Rodney refused to go to Foley High School any longer. He said that he wanted to graduate from Fairhope High School, so I had to leave Pleasure Island after all these years of fun in the sun. I had so much fun, enough for ten people in a lifetime, maybe more. If it was not for Rodney wanting to move to Fairhope, I would have stayed and given Mrs. Pill a run for her money and would be a huge thorn in her side when it came to Al. I did keep the two bottles of fine wine she brought me, though, just in case I did want to have a drink every now then with some of Al's past girlfriends. I knew all of them and in later years have become closer than ever due to knowing and loving Al. We all had our cherished stories and memories of the good old days and wild nights with him. I would think of Mrs. Pill and her tight-ass attitude every sip of the way.

Before the move to Fairhope, a developer from Dallas came walking into my office and asked if I was a local and if I could show him around Gulf Shores. He was almost fifty years old, which at the time seemed too old for me, but he was very good-looking and extremely charming. He was an ex-Dallas Cowboys football player, he had been in United States Marine Corps, and he was rich—but most of all, he really liked me a lot, and he was single.

We became great friends, and I helped him promote his new condo development property—which was located next to the Gulf Shores Plantation—to some homeowners and potential investors in our area. He was fun to be with, and he loved spending lots of money on Rodney and me. After I got to know him as a good friend for several months, we started dating. He had his own private Lear jet, and he would fly me and Rodney to his condo in the French Quarter in New Orleans at least a couple of times each month. Rodney and I felt like we were in high cotton now, and we really were living the high life better now than ever before. Dan also had condo developments on the Mississippi Gulf Coast and in the Virgin Islands. He wanted me to travel with him to Europe to promote several of his resort properties he needed investors for in Germany, France, and Switzerland. It was going to be a trip of a lifetime, first class all the way. I was able to take time off from my job in Gulf Shores and take the trip with him for about two weeks. Rodney was old enough at age fifteen to either stay with Mom and Dad or have some of his friends stay at our house with him.

To this day, Rodney's memory of me leaving for this trip to Europe with Dan is far different from what I remember it being. In Rodney's version, he jokingly says that I gave him twenty dollars and left him with a vat of chicken and rice. Rodney says that I told him, "I'll see you when I get back!" The way I remember it was that Dan gave Rodney two hundred dollars, a new boom box, and let Rodney use his new Jeep Wagoner for the entire two weeks we were gone, because he knew that Rodney already had his own car that I bought him when he turned fourteen, and he was already driving. I also told Rodney that I was sorry I couldn't take him with me. I also told him to do his homework and for God's sake don't be smoking, because I would have friends coming by to check on him every other day. Rodney worked at Burger King (where I once caught him smoking) after school, and he also had a part-time job working at the local amusement park on weekends, mostly during the summer, when the tourists would flock to Gulf Shores. I asked Rodney if it was fun operating the rides like the Tilt-A-Whirl. I'd thought all this time he was working there that this was his job title. He said to me in his calm inside soft voice, "Mama, I wish I could operate the rides, but instead I clean up the vile vomit from all the people who ride the rides." I felt bad that he even had to work, but he wanted to, and as far as I knew, it kept him out of trouble.

One evening at a local hangout named Easy Street—which was owned by none other than Big Al—Dan and I attended a fashion show that for once I wasn't in. I made a comment to Dan that I loved the outfit that one of the models was wearing. After the show, Wesley Burger came over to our table and told me that I could come by the next day to his boutique and pick up all of my new clothes that "Dan the Man" had bought for me. He did not just buy me that one outfit—he bought me every outfit in the entire fashion show. When I asked him why, he simply said that I would need some new clothes for our upcoming trip to Europe. My mouth dropped open as I sincerely thanked him for all his kindness and generosity. I felt like I was falling in love with an older man, and it felt so good. He was falling in love with this hard-working small-town country girl from Gulf Shores, Alabama. I had not traveled at all, other than where my job had taken me throughout the United States—never to Europe. I was so excited about the trip because I knew that I probably wouldn't have an opportunity like this ever again.

One of the most romantic moments we spent together before the trip to Europe was on a trip to Miami where Dan had set up a meeting with Julio Iglesias to buy some property from him and his brother. I was so excited about getting to meet Julio. I had always loved his music; his voice was as smooth as silk, and I loved the song that he had recorded with Willie Nelson, "To All the Girls I've Loved Before." The meeting went well that night with Julio's brother, who was also very good-looking, but it was a no show with Julio. After his meeting, we went to a fine restaurant in South Beach where we ate outside on a beautiful balcony. The weather was perfect with a full moon and a warm Miami breeze, and it was just the two of us. He could tell that I was disappointed about not getting to meet Julio Iglesias. He told me that, to make it up to me, he would sing to me. He began singing, "When I fall in love, it will be forever," and he knew every word to that song. He even had a good singing voice, to my surprise! It was by far the most romantic moonlit moment I have ever had with an older, tall, dark, and handsome Italian man. I could feel the love in his voice and see it in his dark brown eyes when he looked at me. He was truly the tall, dark, and handsome man I was looking for, and as a bonus, he was very rich too. He was so good to me and seemed to love Rodney as well. If we were to get married, I would have been his fifth wife, and he would have been my third husband—and I was only in my late thirties and he had just turned fifty. I liked dating him, but I still had my doubts about marriage to him or to anyone again due to my bad experiences with my last two husbands.

When we arrived in Europe, it was in the winter with lots of snow, and our first stop was Geneva, Switzerland. We stayed at the best five-star hotel there, first-class all the way. It was the Hotel d'Angleterre, built in 1872, and although it was in the financial district of Geneva, it was also within walking distance of all the good shopping that Geneva had to offer. In my spare time, Dan would give me his credit card and tell me to have a good time. Since I never took advantage of moments like that, he let me keep the card, and I gave it back to him when we returned to the United States. Even in the dead of winter in Geneva and in every shop, hotel, and restaurant, there were fresh flowers everywhere. I can only imagine how beautiful it must have been in the spring and summer, especially in all the public parks throughout the city. I was able to even get as many massages as I wanted when I wasn't helping Dan with his meetings held at our hotel. Massage therapy in Europe was as common as us Southern girls getting our hair done every week on a regular basis.

After Geneva, we took what looked like the Orient Express train to Frankfurt, Germany. We had a private car on the nicest train, the kind I had only seen and heard about in the movies and on TV, and here I was riding it with Dan the Man. During the entire trip, I could not believe this was real and not a dream, but it was real and he was real. I was so happy after so many years of being lost and unhappy. When we arrived in Frankfurt, we stayed at the InterContinental hotel, and as soon as we checked in both of us went to the spa for a long relaxing massage. It was there that I was introduced to the European version of hydro-therapy (which today I use in my unique massage technique at my spa) using the heavy layers (at least three) of hot heavy Turkish plush towels from head to toe. They kept the towels in huge wooden vats with ringers like you would see on an old-time washing machine, but they were huge and medieval looking. The water smelled heavenly, as if it had flowers floating in it.

After Dan's business was over in Frankfurt we went on to Hamburg, Germany, where we stayed at another InterContinental hotel on Lake Alster with a view of the Swiss Alps. We ended our long trip in the south of France, where Dan the Man had saved the best for last. It was in the village of Menerbes at the Hotel La Bastide De Marie, which only had sixteen rooms. The hotel was surrounded by its own private vineyard, so every meal we ate there was accompanied by the best of the best of their own wine grown on the property. With snow still on the ground and lots of it, every hotel we stayed at had down comforters on the soft high beds. The large windows had no screens—there was no need for screens even in the summer because they had no bugs. The beautiful windows would open so easily if the room got too hot, so that I could reach out the window and feel the snow on the window ledge. Snow was something that is only dreamed about in south Alabama, so I loved touching it, walking in it, and playing in it as often as I could. After we left the charming quaint hotel in the south of France, we flew home to the United States.

As nice as it was in Europe, when we returned, all I wanted to do was kiss the ground. I realized how spoiled we were by our lifestyle that we all take for granted. I wouldn't trade it for anything, because we have it all here in the good old USA. Seeing my son and my sweet home in Alabama on West Beach Boulevard sitting there, I told myself that I had all the things I needed to make me happy. I thanked Dan for a trip of a lifetime before he left to go back home to Dallas, and right before he left he told me that he loved me more than ever due to us spending those two wonderful weeks together. How sweet it was to hear those words from such a wonderful giving man who opened up a whole new world for me far away from the Redneck Riviera. My trip was again another Forrest Gump moment for being in the right place at the right time, falling into the arms of Dan the Man! In Linnie's World, I believed that his strong arms would hold me tight, close to him forever, and that he would always be there for me and for Rodney, too!

The following month we were off again on Dan's jet to Las Vegas, where a limo picked us up in style, and we stayed at the Riviera Hotel in a suite. The city of lights was so fascinating to me that we rode up and down the Las Vegas strip for an hour so that I could see it all. Dan was a high roller in Las Vegas and also in Atlantic City. He would give me five hundred dollars to play the slots, and every time I would run out of money, he would give me five hundred more, over and over again. Instead of being practical and putting that money in my pocket and taking it home to pay bills, I acted like the blue baby again and just kept taking his money and letting the slots eat it up, as long as he was giving it to me. How stupid was that? It never crossed my spoiled rotten mind that one day the free ride might come to an end, or he might run out of money and not be there for me anymore! I couldn't believe how much I loved playing the slot machines, and I could hardly pull myself away from them. In Linnie's World, I just knew that with the next pull of that handle on the slot machine I was going to win the million-dollar jackpot, but as lucky as I was, that never happened. To this day, I have never returned to Las Vegas, and I have heard from everyone who goes to my famous city of lights that I wouldn't recognize it, with all the glitz and glamour of the new hotel resort casinos that line the strip today.

Dan would fly me back to Gulf Shores after each trip, and he would go back home to Dallas. One weekend we met in Biloxi at one of his many condos, and little did I realize that sadly it would be our last weekend together. I remember that date because it was January 28, 1986. It was again another Forrest Gump moment. That morning, the news came on television that the Challenger space shuttle had blown up in midair. It was our last time together, because the following week he was killed in the Virgin Islands when his private Lear jet went down in the ocean. He had wanted me to go with him, but because Rodney and I had the move to Fairhope ahead of us I didn't go. The move to Fairhope saved my life, and although I was so sad from losing Dan, I knew my life would go on without him. The time we had together was so special to me and to Rodney, and he will always have a special place in my heart forever. I went from being a small-town country girl from Gulf Shores, Alabama, living on the Redneck Riviera, to a well-traveled woman who was lucky enough to be loved, pampered, and spoiled by Dan the Man. I will cherish and miss our wonderful times together. He was a kind, loving man who loved me and loved Rodney, and he changed our lives forever. He spoiled both of us and opened our eyes up to a world that we could have never imagined. He introduced us to the finer things that life has to offer when you have a lot of money and know how to spend it! On those long lonely nights without him, I would truly miss being in the strong arms of Dan the Man.

Chapter 5

MOVING TO FAIRHOPE AND STARTING OVER AGAIN

One month before Rodney and I moved back to Fairhope, I took a few days to fly to New York, where I had received a personal invitation from one of my favorite homeowners who I had met and worked with when I was on the condo resort property in Atlantic City named the Enclave. Her name was Jean Nidetch, and we became instant friends when I loaned her my personal blow dryer. That was one accessory we didn't provide for our new homeowners, and since she was from New York City, she couldn't believe how nice we were being in the South. She told me that she only knew two real Southern people—one was me and the other was her limo driver in New York City, who was from South Carolina. She thought that a few days in the big city would do me good. She said that I could take some time with her to have fun and not think about the death of my friend and lover Dan.

This was the second time I would visit New York City. The first time was when Rodney and I took the casino bus for ten dollars each way from Atlantic City to the Port Authority in New York City. We walked everywhere and saw the city on a poor man's budget, but we had the best time of our lives. It was also one of the most relaxing moments Rodney and I ever had. I had an epiphany while sitting on a park bench next to the big lake in Central Park, looking at the swans swim by as the wind blew the weeping willows all around us. We were so tired from all the walking we had done, and we'd also rented bikes and rode bikes through the park. I asked Rodney to just give me twenty minutes to rest. I laid my head on his shoulder and ask him not talk or say a word to me, and he let me rest and relax to the soft sounds of Central Park and the city in the background. This picture of us sitting there was burned in my mind's eye. I was able to capture that moment and paint it on canvas. The picture of the most relaxing moment of my life now hangs in my bedroom at Rodney's historic home in midtown Atlanta. It was the first epiphany I had ever experienced. I'm so lucky I have it in living color and can touch it and remember that day we spent together in one of my favorite cities of all, New York City.

Jean lived in a three-and-a-half-million-dollar penthouse on Fifth Avenue that overlooked Central Park. It had over three thousand square feet in it. My guest room was almost as big as our original little beach house in Gulf Shores. Since I was without a job, or should I say between jobs, at this point, I thought maybe I could look for something up there. Little did I realize how much it cost to live in New York City, but in Linnie's World, what was money anyway as long as I could pay my bills and take care of Rodney? All I knew was that I couldn't make ends meet at that time in my life, much less rent an apartment in New York City.

Jean and I would start our mornings off drinking coffee and eating breakfast in her huge kitchen. She had any and every kind of frozen Weight Watchers food stored in her high-end Viking stainless-steel freezers that stretched across one long wall of her kitchen. At lunch, we always ate out, and we ate out for dinner at night. She loved to eat lunch at small, quaint little sidewalk café outdoor-type places. Jean Nidetch was the original founder of Weight Watchers—another Forrest Gump moment. Everyone knew her, and she always took lots of time to stop and hear their stories of how she was helping them lose weight because her diet was working for them. When I shared with her that one day I wanted to write a book about being divorced on the Redneck Riviera, she encouraged me in every way. She told me if she could do it and sell over two million copies the first year, then anyone could do it. She was very humble about her life and told me that she used to sell eggs door to door and her husband was a bus driver. When she came up with this diet stuff that worked, people loved it. To this day, she still gets 10 percent of every Weight Watchers place that opens in the world. She loved the title *Divorced on the Redneck Riviera* and thought that alone would sell me some books. Thank God I didn't write the book back then, because I did not have near the material I have now, plus the other two husbands to make it complete might just make it a best seller. Who knows, it might just make a real funny movie with Kathy Bates playing the part of Mama!

In her private limo with her driver from South Carolina, we would go shopping to places that I had only heard about on television like Macy's, Tiffany's, and Brooks Brothers. It was like a dream come true that I was in these stores, and she was spending money like it was what she was meant to do every day. All I did was look and learn how it's really done when you have a lot of money to spend. She bought all kinds of gifts for her daughter and grandchildren. She was such a good hostess in every way and made me feel welcome and at home with her. She was able to get me a hair appointment at the famous Louis and Vincent Hair Salon. Vincent had done her hair for years. He had an appointment just for me at her request because Beverly Sills, the famous opera singer, had cancelled and I was able to take her place—yet again, a Forrest Gump moment of being in the right place at the right time. They even served us wine and cheese after we left the shampoo area. This was a far cry from the beauty shop my gay friend Eddie owned in Gulf Shores. Little did I realize that by the time I walked out of that beautiful salon, I had spent $177 for cut, color, and hairdo, but it was Jean's treat. My friend Eddie was looking better and better for only $50, which was a lot back then for me to spend on my hair. I really felt like a million dollars when I walked out of that fancy salon looking like Linda Evans in Linnie's World.

When I began my walk back to Jean's apartment, I made a quick visit to see someone who I had always wanted to meet, since I was there standing in front of the General Motors Building. On the thirty-seventh floor of that building was the home office for Estee Lauder. I had used her facial products for most of my adult life. I just had to meet her in person to tell her what a good job she was doing for women like me who live on the beach and stay in the sun all the time. When I arrived at her office, a young pretty woman behind the reception desk asked me if I needed some help. When I asked her if I could meet Mrs. Estee Lauder, she looked at me like I was a crazy woman just let out of the crazy house. She told me to stay right there, and she would be right back with someone to help me as soon as she could.

When she returned, she had several employees with her. They all asked why I wanted to meet Mrs. Estee Lauder. I told them that I had three reasons why I wanted to meet her. The first reason was, for many years I had used her wonderful products and since I live on the Alabama Gulf Coast in Gulf Shores, I was living proof that the products work. I was always in the hot sun and always had a good tan by April, but no sun damage to my face due to her full-face heavy foundation makeup that I wore every day. The second reason was, at this point I was between jobs, and if they had an opening I might be interested in joining the Estee Lauder family. I told them that I would make the perfect Estee Lauder spokesmodel on their TV commercials. The third and last reason was, I had just left the Louis and Vincent Hair Salon, where I just paid $177 to get my hair done, and I felt like a million dollars and just had to show it off to her.

After all of their mouths dropped wide open, they walked away and brought back a nice beautiful young lady named Valerie. I told her my reasons for wanting to meet her boss, and she told me that if Mrs. Lauder was not in Europe and if she were right here, right now, those were three of the best reasons she had ever heard for meeting her boss. Valerie happened to be second in line to Estee Lauder at their home office. She was nice enough to take me around and show me the office of Estee Lauder, which was pale baby blue, lots of heavy baby blue velvet drapes, and beautiful antiques from all over the world. I even got to sit in her chair at her desk, and all I could think of was, *Mama, look at your very own blue baby now!* Mama, bless her heart, would have loved seeing Estee's office too, and I wished so many times she could have been with me on so many of my adventures of being in the right place at the right time, especially on that day. Valerie also took me to other floors and gave me a huge Estee Lauder gift bag full of samples of some of the new products they were coming out with. Having the nerve of Dick Tracy, I asked her if I could have two more bags, one for Jean and of course one for Mama, and she said yes. When I left, she and the others told me that in the history of Estee Lauder, no one had ever come right off the street to meet Mrs. Lauder, much less tell them that they were doing a good job and she loved their products. They also said that if I ever came back to New York, to be sure and come by to say hello, and maybe next time Mrs. Lauder might be there so I could tell her myself in person. So far, I haven't had a chance to do that yet, but who knows—my next visit I might get to meet her or her CEO and visit with her staff again like old home week. Miss Valerie was so nice to do all that for me, and it made this south Alabama girl from the Redneck Riviera feel so special that day. I almost felt like a queen for a day, or close to it anyway!

When I got back, I told Jean my story of what a wonderful afternoon I had. She could not believe I did that until I showed her all the stuff they loaded me up with, and I handed her the gift bag that I had gotten for her. I told her that she needed to go by there sometime and ask for Miss Valerie and tell her Miss Linnie from Fairhope, Alabama, sent her. They might just give her some more free stuff, too. Jean told everyone my story when we went out to dinner later that night. We loved eating at a quaint small dinner theater that had a Broadway show. After dinner and the show, all the actors would come over to our table and talk to her. She not only made me feel special, but she made everyone she met feel special, too. The day before I left to come back home to Alabama, she told me that she wanted me to go with her to pick up two new fur coats that her furrier had made for her in the garment district. I had always loved clothes and had been a model for many years in Gulf Shores. I couldn't wait to see what it was like going to the actual garment district in New York City! When we arrived, her furrier had two beautiful coats ready for her to try on. I noticed that she had brought a mink coat with her, and she asked him if he could turn it into a bomber jacket for her. He quickly said no way! He asked her to please not cut up that beautiful, black diamond, three-quarter-length mink coat. He suggested she just give it away or sell it, but not to ask him to cut it up for her. She turned around, looked at me, and said, "Linnie, do you want to buy a mink coat?" Real quick I told her that there was no way I could ever afford a nice coat like that. She then said, "How about seven hundred dollars, and you can pay me fifty dollars a month until you pay it off." I was in shock with happiness and surprise. I told her that it was a deal and to this day, I still have the very first mink coat that Jean Nidetch ever owned with her name in it. It is as beautiful now as it was then. In south Alabama, it hardly ever gets cold enough to wear a mink coat, except to a Mardi Gras ball in the winter every now and then. I wear it with pride and a big smile on my face every time I think about my friend Jean from New York City. What a wonderful adventure that trip was for me, seeing it through the windows of her limo and from the kindness of her big heart.

When I returned to Fairhope with my new mink coat on and showed it off to Mama, the first thing she said was, "Where in the hell did you get that mink coat, and I hope to hell you didn't steal it." I knew then I was back to the real world of Linnie Delmar thanks to Mama. I was ready to take on the world until Mama brought me down a notch or two and back to the reality of being home in Alabama again. That sure was a life I could only visit that one time and dream about for the rest of my Forrest Gump life. I was not about to let Mama get me down after a trip like that. I also gave her the bag of free products that I had received from Miss Valerie. Mama used Estee Lauder products, and when I told her the story of how I got those free products, all she did was shake her head and give me that look. All she could say to me was, "I knew you had the nerve of Dick Tracy, and I hope you had fun because now you have got to find a job." My job had played out with the Gulf Shores Plantation, and the developers had gone bankrupt and out of business. I had to get serious about finding another job. I would certainly miss traveling all over the United States and staying at those premier resort properties for weeks at a time. Most of all, I would miss working with all the wonderful people I met on a daily basis and miss my dear friend Macy.

Jean called me to make sure I got home safely and asked me if I remembered the name of a man that she and I had met in line while trying to get tickets to see the Joan Rivers show in Atlantic City one evening when she and I went out. This was before I was her houseguest in New York. I told her the story of when we saw him at the Golden Nugget at the crap table, and since he thought I looked very lucky, he wanted me to roll the dice for him. I ended up rolling all the right numbers for him for over twenty-five minutes and won the man more than $21,000. For winning him all that money, he gave me $700 and $100 for Rodney as a bonus. I had no idea who he was, much less remembered his name. She told me that she thought he was the owner of the famous Home Shopping Network because she had seen him on TV. Again, a Forrest Gump gambling moment! She asked why and how could I be so lucky to always be in the right place and the right time?

She also reminded me to send her my fifty each month for buying her mink coat, and I assured her I wouldn't miss a payment. She also told me to keep in touch with her and not to forget to write my book *Divorced on the Redneck Riviera*. She said, "With your good luck, it might turn out to be a best seller." I got to thinking about what she said about me being lucky and being in the right place at the right time more than once. Little did I know that the best was yet to come!

I knew it was time to get serious and find a really good job so that Rodney and I could get on our feet again. For a short time, we were living with Mama and Dad at their home on Mobile Bay in Point Clear. This was before we found a cute little cottage on White Avenue, and although it was great living with them, we liked having our own place that we could finally call home. After living on the beach for all those years, I truly missed the smell of the Gulf of Mexico and the sound of the waves that put me to sleep every night. I would also miss the moonlight as it shined in my living-room windows on each side of my fireplace, especially in the winter when I would have a huge fire going and the glare of the fire would reflect off my mirrors on my bedroom ceiling from the living room. If those mirrors could only talk, the sordid stories they could tell! God, I miss those mirrors so much. I was trying to forget about Al, and Dan the Man from Dallas, and get on with my new, simple, boring life in Fairhope. The beautiful memories were still there in living color almost every night. The nights were getting longer and longer, and I didn't have any signs of a new man being in my life anytime soon. I tried to stay focused on getting a job, but I did miss having sex because I liked it so much. I admit that although I had never smoked or taken drugs or smoked pot, sex was my weakness. It was my drug of choice because it made me feel so good every time I had it!

My first job search was a successful one. I rode down to the Grand Hotel Marriott in Point Clear to ask for a job. In Linnie's World, instead of going through the human resource department like a normal person would do, I felt lucky that day. I was hell-bent on talking to the person in charge, the general manager. So, with no appointment, I went to his office to try to get in. I told myself that if I could go in to see Estee Lauder, how hard could it be to get in to see the general manager of the Grand Hotel Marriott? His executive assistant stopped me in my tracks and quickly told me to go sit down. In her official loud voice, she told me that if he had a few moments after his meeting I could talk to him in person, but only for five minutes.

As I took my seat, I heard a kind, soft-spoken man ask me if I was looking for a job. I looked up into the kind face of the Southern gentleman sitting next to me. He introduced himself as Mr. Ollie. He was also waiting to talk to the general manager like I was. Something told me that he wasn't looking for a job like I was, though. He told me that if I needed a job he would hire me, because he needed an executive assistant. I gave him my resume and as we talked. Once again, I knew that I was in the right place at the right time.

He was very famous in our area, and he owned a lot of large grocery stores throughout the Southeast. Of all places, here he was sitting next to me in the general manager's office at the Grand Hotel Marriott. I never made it into to see the general manager, because I now had a new job as executive assistant to Mr. Ollie. He told me to show up for work at my new job on Monday. I was so excited that I couldn't wait to get home and tell Mama the good news. When I told her who I would be working for and how much I would be making, all she did was give me that look and say, "I'll believe it when I see it. I hope to hell you at least know how to type."

All I could do was smile and say, "Thanks, Mama." Again, I felt like the blue baby, but at least I was a happy blue baby with a brand-new job that I was looking forward to, smiling all the way to the bank.

At the time he hired me, Mr. Ollie had just taken office as the chairman of the board for the Chamber of Commerce for the United States. He would assume this title for only one year. First, I was able to organize and redecorate his Mobile office and his sister's office that was next to his. Most of my duties were to handle his real-estate investments and arrange all of his personal appearances and photo shoots for his position with the national Chamber of Commerce in Washington, D.C. He also depended on me to write some of his speeches and to brief his wife on her duties as the chairman's wife. She also had meetings to attend, and I wanted her to always be at the top of her game as much as possible. Most of the time, she did not know what to make of this so-called executive assistant who earned more money than she thought I was worth. It must have been the blue eyes, because it took a while for her to warm up to me. Finally I gained her trust and confidence; she knew I was watching out for her, and I had her blind side covered. She also realized that I had her and Mr. Ollie's best interest at heart first and foremost.

It was not long before the three of us would end up in our nation's capital. For me—and for them, too—to be actually "on the hill" was like country come to town. As soon as everyone heard our (especially my) Southern drawl, they assumed we were Southern and stupid. We were ready, willing, and able to handle anything we had to do to accomplish our goal and get our work done. I wasn't exactly sure what that goal was yet or what we needed to do, but I was willing to find out and do the best job I could do for Mr. Ollie. To my shock and surprise, doors began to open for the both of us, and we were welcomed with open arms into a world that was new to both of us. We loved all the attention! They loved Mr. Ollie, and it became a package deal—if you get him you get me too, and they loved it! We would have one meeting after another with famous people such as Patrick Buchanan; Don Hodel, who was the secretary of the interior; Maureen Reagan, the president's daughter; and Bill Marriott, who was one of Mr. Ollie's biggest fans and supporters and best friends. We were constantly in high gear, and I was like a buzz saw never slowing down because Mr. Ollie would get so pumped up and in turn I stayed pumped up too. Mr. Ollie, during a session with guest speakers for the national Chamber of Commerce, would literally run up to meet them. At times, he was stopped by the Secret Service when it was someone like President Reagan giving a speech. He got so excited just being in the same room with the president. After all, Mr. Ollie was the chairman of the board of the Chamber of Commerce for the United States, so let's hope he was not going to be arrested for running up to someone, even if it was the president of the United States. I would grab him by the arm, more than once, and whisper to him to slow it down to a trot, have fun, and play nice with his new buddies, the big boys on the hill.

He was one of the few people I have ever known without a mean bone in his body. That still holds true to this day. He has always been a true Southern gentleman in every way, and people are drawn to him like a magnet because of his soft voice and kind ways, but most of all his great sense of humor. He was the best boss I could have ever wished for, and he always treated me with kindness and respect. Washington, D.C., loved him, and he was in his glory when he was up there for the year he served as chairman.

He taught me a lot about how it works on the bureaucratic ladder, working your way up to the head office, moving from one office to another to finally get to the top, then starting all over again. Of course, this was all at the taxpayers' expense, and the moving never stopped. I saw it in action when he took me to the Rayburn Building and the world-famous Pentagon. When I tried to ask them why they do it this way, all they would tell me was that this is the way they have always done it here in Washington, D.C., and no one has ever tried to buck the system. It has always been done like this forever. I can't imagine what they must have thought of me and Mr. Ollie—especially me, rebel that I am, always ready to buck the system. We lived on the edge every day due to minute-by-minute plans, rules, and formats that changed like the wind. Most of the time, we tried to follow the bureaucratic bullshit rules, but somehow if we failed it was okay because we were from Alabama. "Just let us hear you talk" would be the first thing they said to us. They loved it, and we saved our asses many a time by just being sweet and talking to them and telling them we were sorry if we screwed up something.

I realize now that there are actually only 545 people who have any say-so or power to make things happen in our government, and they are 100 senators, 435 congressmen, 1 president, and 9 Supreme Court justices—a total of 545 human beings out of 300 million people who are directly, legally, morally, and individually responsible for the domestic problems that plague our country today. The president has the say-so to propose a federal budget. The House of Representatives has the authority to vote on appropriations. Congress has the right to write the tax code and to set fiscal policy, and the Federal Reserve Bank has control of monetary policy. Who would have thought that Mr. Ollie and I would be in our nation's capital of Washington, D.C., where all this stuff happens each and every day? We both were learning a lot during our time spent up there, and it wasn't a pretty sight to see how much money was wasted through the federal government's spending habits.

Although we had a full, busy schedule, we somehow found the time to get pampered. We would usually go to the Watergate Health Club and Spa to get massages. Mr. Ollie's wife was good at being spoiled rotten in a spa just like we were. I had forgotten how good the life of the rich and famous was; when Dan the Man died, my days of getting pampered died too, and the real life set in. The real life in Washington, D.C., was not all bad because of my new employment with Mr. Ollie. We stayed in the finest hotels like the Hay-Adams and the Washington Grand Hotel, and of course with having Mr. Bill Marriott as one of Mr. Ollie's best friends, we stayed at his suite at the Washington Marriott Hotel, and that certainly had some perks that came with it.

All good things must come to an end, and before leaving and going back home to Rodney, Mama, Dad, and my boring life in Fairhope, I had a very special visit to the Pentagon. I actually got to sit at Colin Powell's desk, because no one ever stopped me from walking the halls and sightseeing. I even had a camera hanging around my neck taking pictures all over the Pentagon building. I guess I looked official due to my pass clipped to me. It was my day off and an unexpected trip, so I didn't wear my usual business suit. It was summertime in Washington, D.C., and it was hot as hell. I had on my black halter top and white shorts. It couldn't have been the outfit that got me in for sure, because it was far too casual. It had to be the pass Mr. Ollie gave me and told me to wear at all times, so I clipped it to my black halter top and walked right in like I owned the place. Anyway, everyone was real nice to me and never once asked me who I worked for, or asked the really big question, which was, "What in the hell are you doing here and why?"

I was walking the halls that all looked the same and was thinking about Mama roller skating down these same hallways when she used to work there. I suddenly saw that I was standing right in front of Colin Powell's office, and no one was in there. I walked in and sat down in his office at his desk. While I was looking at all his stuff on his desk, I picked up his phone and dialed nine for an outside line and called my little buddy down in Gulf Shores, Alabama. When wild, wonderfully wicked Wanda answered the phone, I told her, "You will never believe where I'm sitting right now."

The first thing she said was, "What in the hell are you doing up in Washington, D.C., of all places?"

I laughed when I told her she sounded just like Mama, and I would fill her in on the details when I had a little more time to talk. I told her that I had to go because I was going to find the press room and stand at the podium that has the presidential seal on it where President Regan makes all his speeches from in front of the blue velvet curtain. I told her good-bye and "call you later." I hung up before I got caught and got the hell out of there. I finally found the press room, and I got someone to take my picture standing in front of the blue velvet drapes where President Regan makes all his speeches when he's at the Pentagon building. The picture turned out good, and the presidential seal was next to where I was standing. I got a good picture of that, and the person who took the picture never asked me—not once—what in the hell I thought I was doing there. How and why I never got arrested or at least questioned as to why I was there is still a question I will never know the answer to. I may have acted official, but I sure as hell didn't look official that day, so it must have been the pass Mr. Ollie gave to me that allowed me that kind of freedom!

My job with Mr. Ollie had come to an end, and what an experience it was for him and for this country girl who had just come from the Redneck Riviera and ended up on the hill in our nation's capital rubbing elbows with the president of the United States due to my wonderful boss and dearest friend Mr. Ollie!

When I returned to Fairhope, I told Mama some of my encounters and adventures while in Washington, and all she could say was, "Girl, you have the nerve of Dick Tracy, and they could have thrown you under the jail for taking all those pictures at the Pentagon, you ought not had done that." She had firsthand knowledge of how tight security was at the Pentagon building since she used to work there in her younger days, but knowing Mama, I'm almost positive she wasn't wearing a black halter top and white shorts. She said, "I thank God you're finally home to stay, I hope?" Rodney had missed his mama, and I sure missed him too. I was lucky that he enjoyed staying with Mama and Dad during all the months I was gone.

Rodney was so happy to get to go to school at Fairhope High School. He had made lots of new friends and was going into the tenth grade. The year was 1986, and with no job in sight because Mr. Ollie's one-year term was up, I knew I needed to get a trade and maybe start my own business. Of all the things I could have picked, I decided to get as much schooling as I could and become a Licensed Massage Therapist (LMT). It seemed to be a good fit for me and a job that I was made for. Mama said that when I was a child, I would grab people and start rubbing their feet or back and think nothing of it. I would also be the first massage therapist in Fairhope. Mama and Dad supported me in my decision and helped pay for all the advanced training I would need to work with doctors and world-class resorts. I physically worked hard, and for the first time in a long time, I was focused on what I needed to do to be the best at something.

I was ahead of my time, because when I told some of my local Fairhope friends what I was going to do, they thought I was crazy and that I would never make it due to the sexual comments it implied. I had gotten massages in Europe and in Washington, D.C., and all over the United States when I was working at all the resorts where I was manager of customer service, and I knew that I had finally found my calling and my niche.

After all my advanced training, and after I received my license as an LMT, the first place I went to drum up some business was the Grand Hotel Marriott in Point Clear. I knew that there were people staying there from all over the world. The first thing they would want, after checking into the hotel, would be a good massage. When I went to the general manager to discuss what I wanted to do, he looked at me as if I was crazy because he had never had a professional massage before. The Grand Hotel had never provided a massage service, so all of this was new for him. After thinking about it and discussing it with the convention sales department, he gave me the okay.

I had a built-in clientele, and they would even bring the people to me and I would take them back, or the hotel would come pick them up from my cute little cottage in downtown Fairhope. I had my small, quaint cottage made into a day spa before day spas were even heard of. I also had a huge hot tub on my gated back deck where clients would relax for fifteen or twenty minutes before their hour-long massage. They got all this for a whopping sixty-five dollars, plus they would always tip me good too! In 1986, that was a lot of money to get pampered for an hour-long professional massage. I felt like I was finally going to have my own successful business, and Rodney and I were going to make it. He was happy that I was an LMT because I would use him as my guinea pig; every time, I would learn something new. To this present day, he still gets massages on a regular basis in midtown Atlanta to help him deal with his high-stress job in real estate. He is like his mama—he loves to get pampered as often as possible by getting a good massage.

After I started my massage therapy business and after all of my advanced training and schooling, I had the new beginning I needed to, yet again, start all over again! Also, my overwhelming desire for sex kicked back in and the love of a good man, just one good man, was on my mind a lot. As yet, I had not met anyone who I was attracted to. Mama and Rodney kept telling me that I was too picky, but until I had some special chemistry with someone, I wasn't ready to settle for just anyone. Of course, from time to time, I still had the urge to cross that big bridge onto Pleasure Island and go back home to the Redneck Riviera and get my Big Al fix. God was driving the bus again, and I was over being involved with a married man, so I never took that drive down to Gulf Shores.

I never saw Al again until over twenty-one years later at a party. It was in the present day and time, I was pushing sixty, and he was in his mid-sixties, and it was by accident that we ran into each other at a private party in Gulf Shores. I had no idea he was going to be there, and he had no idea I was going to be there. When we came face to face after twenty-plus years and our blue eyes met, we stood there and talked for almost two hours, and then said good-bye to a lot of good memories. We both knew there was no going back to our old wild ways, and we both knew we had our own separate lives to live. He is still with his same wife who has stood by him all these years. I'm also happy with the special man in my life; we travel all over the United States on our Harley-Davidsons and live life to the fullest each and every day that we can spend together. My motto has always been "Never a dull moment" in the life of Linnie Delmar, and my life even now is anything but dull.

Actually, in 1986, I hardly ever went to Gulf Shores unless I was taking Mama down to check on the five condos she owned in Orange Beach. I was trying to be a good girl!

I was getting tired of staying home on the weekends, so I decided to go out with my girlfriends. We went to a famous bar on the Mobile Causeway named Traders. A good friend of mine, Anna, worked there; she used to model with me in Gulf Shores. She had always wanted me to come by to visit, so we did. I walked in the door and got a drink and sat down. Some good old rock-and-rolls songs were playing on the jukebox. I saw a handsome blond man with a good body and a good tan walking right toward me. Lo and behold, it was my uncle by marriage, from when I was married to my first husband, Donnie. I said, "Hi, Uncle Benny. Where's Aunt Patsy?"

He said in a very soft, sexy voice, "Well, Aunt Patsy and I are divorced now, and what about you?"

I explained to him that I was single again and was taking my time about getting out there again and dating.

He told me right off the bat, "Well, I am out there again, and here you are out there again, so do you want to dance?"

That's when the magic began with "Benny the Candy Man." As my good luck would have it, my very first time out on the town with my girlfriends—"right out of the chute," as my dad would say—and I meet someone who steals my heart and had me at hello! I named him Benny the Candy Man because he sold candy and lots of other items for school fund-raisers. That was his day job, and he was good at it. He was like a magnet to people, especially all the women schoolteachers. They loved him because he was so good looking with a great body. He had the best sense of humor that could make anyone belly laugh at any given time.

He was also a scratch golfer, and he began to teach me everything there was to know about playing golf. When we began dating, we played golf every Thursday afternoon at Lake Forest Country Club, and on weekends we played at the Springhill Country Club. He would bet lots of money with his golfing buddies and always win because he was so good. He made me happy on the golf course during the day and happier at night in the bedroom. The games in both places were more than great, and life was good again.

Both of us were at the top of our game and in our prime. It became harder and harder to keep my mind on my massage therapy business, but somehow I managed both. I was only forty, and I was the best LMT in Fairhope, but also pretty good at golf too. As his lover, he told me that I was the best he had ever had. He loved the women, and they all loved him, so I took that as a huge compliment.

We were not only lovers but also became the best of friends. He was just like me in so many ways, and we could be our crazy selves around each other. I felt comfortable with him because we had known each other since I was eighteen. We had a ball, and we kept each other laughing. We couldn't get enough of each other as lovers and best friends. We were on our way to falling in love with each other, and Rodney hated it. He still liked Uncle Benny, but looked at him as his uncle, and he thought it was sick that I should be dating his uncle. In my mind, since he was my uncle by marriage, I thought it was all right!

I looked at Uncle Benny as one of the most fun-loving men I had ever met, and the sex just kept getting better and better! I had also met a lot of new friends through him, and we had such a good time together. There were about twelve of us who loved playing golf as much as possible. We had cookouts after golfing most every weekend. The months were turning into over two-and-a-half years together.

The most wonderful opportunity came my way when I least expected it. A door was opened for me to get to meet the famous country legend Merle Haggard.

I had a chance to go on the road as his personal LMT. I met Merle at a concert with my girlfriend Gloria. A friend of mine and a client told Merle's manager that I was the best massage therapist he had ever been to. We were invited backstage where we met Merle on his tour bus fondly named "Hag One." I offered my services to him because his back had gone out, and he needed a quick fix. He was so impressed by my technique of neuromuscular therapy that he wanted me to go on the road right then with his East Coast tour. I had to say no because I believed in getting things organized (damn that OCD) before leaving for a long trip like that. I also had to make sure Rodney could stay with Mom and Dad for a few weeks. He said since I couldn't go on this East Coast tour, I could catch up with him later on his West Coast tour coming up in a few months. I told him that would work out better for me and my business, giving me the time to plan and prepare. By saying no to him and not going on with him on his East Coast tour, I missed going to the White House where he put on a private show for George and Barbara Bush. I could have, and probably would have, gotten to work my magic hands on the president and first lady! I could have kicked my OCD ass! All was not lost, because I did go on his West Coast tour a couple of months later for almost a month.

They flew me to Sacramento, California, and it was like country come to town because I was so excited. When they pulled up at the airport to pick me up on Hag One, they looked at all the huge crates loaded with massage equipment and my luggage and gave me a look that I've seen many times from Mama! I knew then I had brought too much stuff and screwed up. I felt like they hated me before I opened my country-ass mouth. When I finally went aboard Hag One and saw Merle, the first thing he said was, "Girl, all I needed was your talented hands. What's up with the luggage and what in the hell is in that huge crate?" I felt like at that moment he hated me, too!

The bus driver/drummer, Biff, told the other band members, "For God's sake, you think we will have room to sleep on the bus tonight with all this stuff?"

Then they all laughed and I felt like we had broken the ice. Merle said, "Get over here and work on my neck, it's killing me."

It was hard work being on his tour bus, but what an experience for me to learn how to be Massage Therapist to the Stars. That is the title the *Mobile Press-Register* newspaper gave me, and it has always stuck. Merle was so nice to me and down to earth, and he was easy to work on. He would usually get a massage treatment before his concert and again early the next morning on the bus while en route to our next concert. It was very hard work, not only for him but for his band and staff who adored him.

It was hard work for me too, and I quickly got over trying to have things organized and perfect for his massage treatments. I had to learn how to work off the cuff at a moment's notice. I got good at it, though, in a hurry! That is the main thing I learned from traveling on the road with him. We started the tour in Sacramento, and the tour ended in Phoenix, Arizona. Along the way, Merle would always stop in Bakersfield where he was from. We always ate at his favorite restaurant. Everyone knew him, and he knew all their names too. Then we went on to a lot of big and small towns along the West Coast where he would play huge concerts, state and county fairs, and rodeos.

He told us one time that this girl who he ran into a lot was a pretty good singer. He said in his calm beautiful voice, "Trisha might just make it big one day." The girl he was talking about turned out to be Trisha Yearwood, and she did make it big. One of the few pictures that he had hanging on Hag One was a beautiful picture of Dolly when she was about eighteen. Like all of us, he loved Dolly! He also asked me if I wanted to play golf with him and Glen Campbell while we were in Phoenix. Like a fool, I said no too quickly, because I had to get my equipment set up to work on some of the other band members. Before I knew it, that one and only chance came and went before I had time to think about it due to my OCD. I could kick my ass again, but then I told myself, who else from the Redneck Riviera that I know has ever been on Hag One with the one and only Merle Haggard? So I didn't throw myself under the bus too bad!

On the bus when it was en route, I was assigned to a small bunk bed that was built into the side of the narrow hallway. I always felt closed in and ended up sleeping on the sofa in the back of the bus in the kitchen area. After each concert, Merle was such a perfectionist that he would watch his taped performance to see if he could improve his smooth-as-velvet voice. When I asked him why he did that, he told me he does that because he loves his fans and without pleasing them he wouldn't be where he is today. He wanted the songs to be perfect, and they were. I remember one song that for some reason I never heard him sing on the radio. It was one of my favorites named "Me and Crippled Soldiers." That song would bring tears to everyone who loves our USA, and he sung it at the end of each of his shows while I was on tour with him. He was smart, funny, very easygoing, and fun to work with. What a special experience for me to get to know him and work for him.

When the tour ended, they flew me back to Mobile. From then on, I was known as the Massage Therapist to the Stars. I rubbed Merle the right way, is the way the *Mobile Press-Register* wrote it up in the local newspaper. Little did I know then that there would be a lot of famous movie stars and singing groups that I would get to rub the right way in the years that followed. I was so proud that the famous Merle Haggard was the very first singer to experience my unique massage technique that I am famous for!

When I returned to Mobile with a pocketful of cash and some brand-new boots that Merle gave me, I was ready to take on the world and see Benny the Candy Man for some good loving. He picked me up from the airport in Mobile, and we were so excited to see each other, we made a stop at his place in Mobile before he drove me across the bay to Fairhope. For hours we made love and also made plans to see each other in the next few days. I was looking forward to the weekend when I would see him again, and we could spend the night together and make love all night to catch up. Being away for almost a month showed me that Benny meant a lot more to me than I had realized. I felt like I was falling in love with him, but as yet I had never told him how I felt.

I unpacked in time to regroup and get my business organized again with my regular clients. It was Saturday night when the phone rang. When I answered it, thinking that it had to be Benny, it was one of my girlfriends, Marilyn, who sounded really upset and serious when she asked me, "Are you sitting down?" When I asked her what was wrong, she told me that Benny had announced last night at Chantilly's (which was our favorite place to go dancing in Mobile) that he and Diane were getting married! I asked Marilyn, "Who in the hell is Diane?" She told me that she had only met the woman once while I was gone out of town, but that Benny had been seeing her the whole time I was on tour with Merle. He had met her at Chantilly's and she too was a good dancer, like me, and she was also a good golfer. All I could do when she told me was scream out, "How could he make passionate love to me one night and say he is getting married three days later to someone else?"

I couldn't believe he could do this to me or to us, but he did, so I called him. When I asked him on the phone, "How can you marry someone you just met when you told me you had missed me and you acted like you were in love with me just the other night?" All he could say was that he had to go because he was going to meet her parents. Before I could say another word, he hung up on me! I tried many times to call him back, just for him to tell me that he did not love me, he loved her. I needed closure, and I needed it bad, for him to just tell me something to that effect would have made the biggest difference in the world to me, but I never talked to him again. After two-and-a-half years of some of the most fun, laughing more than I had ever laughed, and some of the wildest sex I had ever had, I realized I did not know him at all. Who was this man I thought I had fallen in love with? There had never been a dull moment, and we had never had a cross word with each other or an argument.

I was totally heartbroken again and let down by someone who I thought truly loved me and wanted me to be a part of his life because he had been such an important part of mine. I again felt so let down and so lonely with that sick feeling that takes forever to get over. Now that he was taking her around all of our golfing friends, I even lost them as friends too. I was out, and she was in! I guess they weren't my real friends after all like I thought they were. He was a great golfer and people not only loved him for that, but he was so much damn fun and everyone wanted to be around him. I don't blame them for taking his side when it came to our breakup. For months I didn't feel like doing anything or going anywhere because I was so depressed. I missed him, and I missed playing golf, too, but what I missed the most was the sex. Benny the Candy Man would be a tough one to get over, much less replace, but life goes on.

The breakup gave me more time to spend with Rodney and to put forth all my attention on him and on my massage therapy business of being the best LMT I could be. I got to thinking about when I moved to Fairhope and left the Redneck Riviera behind me, that I had met Big Al my first time out on the town and look where that got me. Now years later, living here in my hometown of Fairhope, my first time out on the town

I met Benny the Candy Man. Now look where that got me! I thought to myself, *It must be me*. What am I doing, falling for and dating these guys, guys who I thought were or just might be The One, and they both let me down completely as boyfriends. They let me down as men who I thought I knew and trusted. What was I doing wrong for this to happen now for the second time, once with Donnie, and now with his uncle, Benny the Candy Man? I had my mind made up that the next time would be different, and if and when I met someone, I would take my time to get to know him first as a good friend before I slept with him. That was my plan, and I was sticking to it!

The months seemed to drag by, especially the weekends with no date in sight. So since I had some time on my hands, I began to improve my cute little cottage. I painted it a soft pastel pink with white trim, and of course I had to have the white picket fence and lots of flowers planted everywhere. It was so warm and so cute that Rodney and I truly had made a house into a home again here in Fairhope. I was comfortable with my business in my home and welcomed everyone with open arms. I still had that itch that needed to be scratched. I still felt like I had to have a man to complete me as a person in order for my life to be complete. I still felt a need to be a couple again with someone out there. Where was he, and why was I still unhappy being alone?

To avoid that lonely feeling, I began to involve myself with the local activities in the Fairhope and Point Clear area, which meant getting to know more about polo and how this amazing game is played. I also became involved with the Ken Stabler Celebrity Golfing Tournament held at the Grand Hotel Marriott every year by volunteering my services. I turned to the man who was the head of the Point Clear Polo Club. His name was Kenny McLean, and he had been a dear friend and a regular client since I started my business. He was the man who was able to introduce me to the elite world of polo on the Eastern Shore. What a world it turned out to be for me then and even in later years of my life.

In our area, if you were involved with polo in any way, it meant that you had money. Most of the fans of polo were pretty well off, except for a few others who were broke like me. Everyone knew I was far from being rich, because I was always working on the players on my high-touch massage chair set up next to the horse trailers at any given match. My friend Helen, who took care of Kenny's polo ponies and still does, made sure I always had a good spot to set up. Kenny wanted to pay me every time for doing the chair massages for his team and even the other team players during a match, but I never accepted any money from him. I would just tell him to send me some business for the hour treatment at my home/business, and that was payment enough. Kenny being a man of his word, that's just what he did. He sent me all the polo players from around the world for over nine years. I have worked on everyone from the Palm Beach Polo Club to a prince from Pakistan to famous polo players from South America and Europe. Every weekend, I was booked up thanks to my dear friend Kenny McLean.

The most famous player he sent to me to work on every day while staying in Point Clear at the Grand Hotel Marriott playing polo for the British polo team was Major Ronald Ferguson, the father of the Duchess of York, Sarah Ferguson. Major Ferguson was chosen by the queen of England from her royal army to teach Prince Charles how to play polo when he was a young boy. Major Ferguson was a fun-loving person just as his daughter is, and we became very dear friends for the more than nine years that I worked on him.

He was a tough old bird, to say the least, and had that dry British sense of humor that only a dear friend could understand. For some reason, we hit it off from day one because I couldn't stand looking at his long—and I mean long—eyebrows that stood straight up. I would always kid him about his eyebrows and joked that one day he just might let me trim them up for him. Of course, that day never came, because he said his huge eyebrows were his trademark. I guess he loved the idea of me having the nerve of Dick Tracy to even mention it to him. He also loved that when I did attend a formal polo event, I was always on the arm of what he called my "good-looking boy toy," who most of the time was at least ten years younger than me and pure eye candy through and through. For some reason, he found that to be his way of getting back at me for the eyebrow thing, so for years we went back and forth with that foolishness.

The last game of polo he played in Point Clear, I can remember well. When he arrived in town to play, he came for his daily massage and complained of a really bad pain in his side. I knew right away that something was wrong; I had never heard him complain before. I got him to get in and relax in the huge hot tub that I had on my back deck of my home/business. I told him not to play the match and just let the young ones play in his place. He told me in his bold low British voice, "I have to play due to all of the people paid a lot of money to see *me* play, not the young ones. After all, it is a fund-raiser for the cancer society." Play he did, the whole match, and they won. He was hurting so bad that he couldn't stay to accept the award. He told me to take him to the hospital because his side was really hurting worse than ever. I put him in my little white convertible with the top down and away we flew to Thomas Hospital.

When he arrived, they were ready for him, so I took care of all the details while they took care of him. The tough old bird was really tough after all, because he had three cracked ribs from playing a match in Rhode Island and had taken a fall, which he failed to tell me. The doctors thanked me for knowing what to do by wrapping him as tight as I could around his waist during the match with a wide Ace bandage. I knew that would help the ribs stay in place more than adding to his discomfort. Although I had no idea that his injury was so serious at the time, I had a gut feeling that it had to be something wrong with his ribs, and it was.

The major thanked me and told me if I ever got over to London to let him know, and he would return the favor. I said to myself, *Like that is ever going to happen—me going to London?* Because of his broken ribs, little did I realize then how bonded our friendship would be years later. To this day, he will always hold a special place in my heart as a dear friend and one of the most famous polo players I have ever worked on and known. The queen could not have picked a better person who loved the game more than Major Ferguson did. He was an excellent player and coach who taught Prince Charles and in later years the prince's two sons with Princess Diana, Harry and the future king of England, Prince William.

My business was growing strong, not only because of working with the Point Clear Polo team, thanks to Kenny, but the Grand Hotel Marriott was sending me all their guests and VIPs, every last one of them. They would bring them to me and I would drive them back in my little convertible with the top down most of the time. Life was good for the first time in a long time, and I didn't have a man in my life ruling me and my every move and emotion. I was feeling more and more confident with myself and much more confident becoming Fairhope's first and best Licensed Massage Therapist. Clerks of the elite shops in Fairhope would usually address me by my first name with a brief hello when I walked in, because I did not fit the preppy Fairhope mold and dress code; most of the time I had on tan slacks, a white golfing shirt with the logo of the Grand Hotel, my nametag, and black flats.

One year during Mardi Gras, I saw a beautiful dress in the showcase window of one of the upscale shops in downtown Fairhope and asked if I could try it on, and the lady told me, after looking at my nametag and what I was wearing, that the dress I wanted was very expensive. I told her I realized that, but I still wanted to try it on anyway. It would be perfect to wear to any formal affair like the annual Grand Summer Ball here in Fairhope or Mardi Gras ball, and I wanted that dress! After I pulled out four hundred dollars in cash, she became so nice to me and her whole snooty attitude changed as she smiled and told me to enjoy my new dress and please come back to see them.

I felt like Julia Roberts in the movie *Pretty Woman*. In the present day, you are most likely to see me in my Harley-Davidson outfits. The second love of my life won't be parked too far away. I ride a Harley-Davidson Ultra Classic Trike I fondly named Big Boy! Back then, though, they would say, "Hey, Miss Linnie, how is your massage parlor doing?" If they only knew how ignorant that sounded to me and to everyone else who knows that massage therapy is second nature to most well-traveled people. They didn't realize that the first thing a person wants to do after checking into a first-class resort hotel such as the Grand Hotel Marriott is to get a relaxing massage. I would smile and reply, "It is going pretty well. The Grand Hotel is good about sending me all their well-traveled guests and movie stars from all over the world." This day and time, those shop owners are my regular clients. How about that for progress in the quaint little town of Fairhope, Alabama, and not very far away from the Redneck Riviera? The local people prove to me each and every day that I picked the right profession as an LMT. If they only knew that for once in my life, I was going by the book and rules of the trade of never compromising my professional integrity.

One day I had a nice surprise arrive at my home/business. I had finished working on a client, and in my waiting area (my living room) sat a man I had never seen before. As usual, I got him to fill out my client information form and then I worked on him. After the treatment, he told me in a soft, low voice that it was by far the best massage he had ever received. He asked me if I was going to the big concert later that night. I asked him what concert? He said it was at Judge Roy Bean's to raise money for the cancer society, and it was being put on by the Point Clear polo team. It was about that time that a big black limo pulled up in my front yard to pick this guy up. When I asked him to tell me what he did for a living, he said he played in a little band named Alabama, and his name was Teddy Gentry. I had no idea who Teddy Gentry was and did not care. To me, he was just another client wanting a massage. That again turned out to be a Forrest Gump moment of always being in the right place at the right time. I told Teddy that there was no way I could pay forty dollars for a ticket to go that concert, and he told me to just bring my high-touch massage chair and tell security I was their new massage therapist, and to send me backstage to their bus and they would be waiting for me. He also said I could bring a friend if I wanted to.

I called one of my girlfriends, Gloria, and told her to get her crazy butt over to my house because we were going to see the group Alabama. I did not tell her that we were getting to go backstage, much less on their tour bus. I wanted to shock the hell out of her like Teddy did me! That turned out to be a great experience and an evening Gloria and I would not soon forget.

When I asked my baby sister Kim "Who is Teddy Gentry?" she yelled out, "I cannot believe you do not know who Teddy Gentry or Randy Owens is." Really, up until the point when I finally heard them sing a couple of songs when I was backstage, I had no clue. Kim was a singer for her group, City Limits, and they were the house band for many years at a huge country bar in Mobile named Austin's. She, unlike me, actually knew about all the country singers and the names of all the singers in the groups. I really could not have cared less. I actually had to go out and buy a tape of Merle Haggard before I went on his West Coast tour to see who he was, because I hardly ever listened to the country-music radio stations.

It also blew her mind when I called to ask her, "Who is Merle Haggard?" I have always loved messing with her like that and still do it as often as I can to keep her on her toes just like Mama does to me.

With my job, every day was new and unusual, working on everyone from A-list movie stars to the guy next door. I loved every moment of it, and it was only getting better as the years went on. Even now, in the present day, I feel the same—and it is still getting better and better as time goes on. Getting older just means that I have to pace myself and not work on as many people a day because I want my last client to feel as good as my first client did.

To learn more about my business back then in 1989, I decided to take another class to learn more techniques of how to improve the relaxation levels of my clients. This meant going to the local mental-health center in Fairhope to sign up for a stress-management class, and of all things, I was signing Mama up, too. If anyone needed a stress-management class to learn how to relax, it was Mama! To this day, she is still my worst client to work on because she has no clue about how to let her muscles go and totally relax. She also talks throughout the whole session, and I have to ask her not to talk but let this be your special time to get pampered and relaxed. I ask her to try to get into the zone and let this be her time to let go and relax. She has no clue what the zone is and could care less about finding out how to get there. I end up begging her to shut up and to please just let me do my job. Less than five minutes later, she is talking again about things like going to Walmart and don't forget to pick up toilet paper, and that is when I feel like choking her. Yet I still offer to work on her almost every week, I guess to punish myself in order to relax her if only for a brief moment; after all she is my Mama. She always says she feels better after a treatment, but I do not understand how when she is talking the whole time. When I asked her if she wanted to go to the stress-management class, she looked at me and said, "Why do I need to go with you? I'm not stressed out." She ended up going with me after all just to see what a stress-management class was, if nothing else. Our first evening class was one I would not soon forget, due to Mama just being Mama. God forbid her keeping an open mind and learning something new.

We had eighteen people in the class, and our teacher asked if we would introduce ourselves and tell the class a little bit about ourselves. Mama and I were the very last two people to talk and tell the class why we were there as they went around the room. The stories we heard from all the class members ranged from people having high-stress jobs and not knowing how to cope, to people who were going through a divorce, to people who were there due to the death of a loved one. All the stories were heartfelt, and a couple of them made me feel like I was going to cry any second. I felt so sad for some of those people having to experience such sadness in their busy lives that added to their stress and their reason for being in that class.

The instructor finally got to Mama. He politely asked her if she would stand up so that everyone could hear her (just like everyone had done before her), and she said no! She was not showing or expressing any emotion or caring about the stories she just heard from the rest of the class. Mama gave the entire class that look that I have seen many times (not attractive at all) and blurted out in her loud outside harsh voice, "I am here because she made me come," and pointed to me.

At this point, you could hear a pin drop! I turned blood red from embarrassment, and in a really nice soft inside voice I said, "Mama, you know you wanted to come."

She said in her loud outside harsh voice again, "No, I didn't want to come, you made me."

After all that was over, the teacher spoke up and broke it up between us by saying, "Well, Marjorie, just tell us a little bit about yourself, and we will move on to our last student, your daughter Linnie."

That's when I got the shock of my life when she said, "My name is Marjorie, that's it."

I said again in a calm soft voice, "Mama, please tell them a little more than that about yourself."

And she said it again, "Marjorie, that's it," and gave me that "go to hell" look that meant leave me the hell alone and move on to the next person, I'm done!

The teacher looked at us with shock and horror on his surprised face and said, "Well, thank you, Marjorie." He gave me that look like *You poor girl, having to deal with Mama every day* and asked me if I would stand up and tell the class why I was there. To break the tension and break the ice and not have the class think we both were nutcases, I said, "Well, the first reason I am here is sitting right next to me, and the second reason is also looking at me as I speak." The teacher and the whole class started to laugh and so did Mama, bless her heart.

Then I told them the real reason I was there was to learn more hands-on techniques about stress management. I wanted to put them into practice on my clients because I was an LMT and owned a massage-therapy business there in Fairhope. I was also thinking to myself that the class might teach me something about why I kept choosing the wrong men who ended up leaving me and I have to start all over again. This class also might teach me more about my OCD and help me deal with it. The class would help me see what I was doing wrong. It might teach me some things to do to improve myself and better deal with my OCD.

Little did I realize at the time that a man sitting across the room from me was about to change my life and rock my world. Meeting him for the first time at the Fairhope Mental Health Center should have been the first red flag that told me, *Don't even think about this man.* The second red flag was the word of a friend of mine named David from Gulf Shores who was in the class. He told me real quick, "Don't mess with that good-looking blond guy, because he's messed up!" I should have listened to him too!

Chapter 6

HUSBAND #3—FALLING IN LOVE WITH RICH

Going to the stress-management class at the mental-health center in Fairhope and taking Mama was a big mistake. She went that night but hated every minute of it and made it hard for me to focus on learning something. I loved the class even with her sitting next to me, giving me that "go to hell" look the whole time. I loved every moment of hearing the interesting stories of how and why these eighteen people wanted to learn how to deal with the stress in their very busy lives. I was ready to learn some hands-on techniques and how to use them in my massage-therapy business and how to help people deal with stress on a daily basis in today's society. I loved hearing the soft new-age music we would listen to at the end of each class while laying on the floor. It helped put me in the relaxation zone. Mama had never visited the zone, and if she let her guard down enough to even get close to the zone, I never knew about it. She was one to never share one thing about her emotions and feelings, much less experience a relaxation zone. My sister Val and I cry our eyes out at sad movies, but Mama and Kim never shed a tear. She also never says anything about her personal life or tells her business to anyone outside our small family, much less to a class of eighteen strangers. To this day, when I give her one of my treatments using my famous unique technique, she talks through the whole massage. God knows I have tried, but I have no clue how or if it will ever happen that I succeed in actually relaxing my mama, bless her heart!

The first class I went to, when I looked across from me, I couldn't help but notice the best-looking man I had ever seen looking back at me. He had thick blond hair, tan skin, blue eyes, white teeth, and the most perfect body I had seen on any man in my life. His name was Rich, and his story was so sad that I almost cried hearing him tell what had happened to him and why he was there.

He was in the process of a nasty divorce, and he wanted full custody of his three-year-old twin boys. He missed being with his kids more than any person I had ever heard of. They meant everything to him. He sounded like he had been a perfect father in every way from the time they were born. He was so upset about his soon-to-be divorce, I knew he probably would not want to think about meeting someone, much less going out on a date. I knew this would be a hard nut to crack—and this nut I met at the Fairhope Mental Health Center, of all places. In Linnie's World, though, I thought, *What the hell, I am going for it because he is perfect for me in every way.* He was a well-educated college graduate from Auburn, had a great job at our local hospital, made lots of money, and was soon to be single.

Those things alone were music to my lonesome ears. Most of all, he was the eye candy that I could see myself spending the rest of my life with! I also told myself that I would start over and dust myself off again since Benny the Candy Man was out of the picture. I was ready to get back on that horse again and ride like hell until I wore another lucky big stud out. After all, I was a good person who loved a good time, and I was tired of my so-called dull life of all work and no play. I still thought I was going to meet the perfect man, fall in love, get married again, and live happily ever after.

At the end of the class, I told Mama she was going to have to drive herself home. I was getting a ride with Rich. When she asked me who in the hell was Rich, I looked in her pretty blue eyes and said, "Rich is going to be my next husband!" She gave me that "go to hell" look again and told me that I really did need this class because I had lost my mind. I had a gut feeling that he was The One that I was going to spend the rest of my life with, and I had just met him only two hours ago. He saw me standing in the parking lot, and when I asked him for a ride home, he smiled and to my surprise told me to get in. When we got to my house, I invited him in for a visit, and we talked for a while to get to know each other better. The first thing he asked me was, "Why did you bring your mother to the class?" I laughed and said that I had been asking myself that same question all night. He said he could tell that Mama was not a person who wanted to share her life story. He had the most beautiful blue eyes, just like mine, and I got lost in them. His lips were perfect and with that hard body, I could not think straight. He was so perfect, my first thought was that he might be gay. That thought quickly left my mind when he kissed me goodnight. I knew then that he could not dare be gay.

As the next three months flew by, we became the best of friends. We got together every chance we could, and he even let me meet his two boys after a month or two went by. The experience of being with his three-year-old boys made me want to be a mother again. It gave me a second chance at motherhood. I might do a better job with them than I did with Rodney when he was that age. I could spend more time with them now that I was self-employed. I felt so guilty that I had let Rodney down in so many ways for not being tuned into his feelings and for leaving him with Mom and Dad so many times due to the jobs I had traveling all over the country. I could not have any more kids of my own. I looked forward to keeping his boys every chance I had. They were the greatest, and they made me feel young again. I was having the time of my life, but Rich was still going through such pain from his recent divorce. He didn't want the divorce, but his wife did. He was still missing his boys more than words could explain. Although I was older than him, it never seemed to matter to him as much as it did to me. I was a very young forty-two and he was a very mature and responsible thirty-two, a ten-year difference. He seemed to like the fact that I was older with a lot of experience. He found that to be sexy. Sticking to my plan of not having sex until we got to know each other as best friends first, it was six long months into the relationship before we were ready to get it on. He also had time to adjust to being divorced and a single dad. I knew how it felt to heal a broken heart, and that time was the best medicine for the intense pain.

Our first time, I remember it like it was yesterday because it was such a romantic evening to remember. We were at my cute little pink cottage in my charming bedroom. I had soft music playing, a very sexy outfit on, and lots of candles and dim lamps so I could see if the wait was worth it. I had to put on a very slow, sensual, "Sue Linda" pole dance for him (his first of many more to come). As we began to take our clothes off, I could not believe my eyes! His body was so perfect, and again as lucky as I am, Rich was so well-endowed and his body was perfect in every way. I told him in a calm, sexy, soft voice that I could live with this pretty thing for the rest of my life, and I really meant it! How could I go through life at age forty-two and never ever have laid eyes on a man with a small dick and a fat body? Up to this point in my life, I had been in more than a few relationships and seen more than a few naked men. Mentally, I ask myself how in the world this little Southern girl, now a middle-aged woman, from the Redneck Riviera could be so lucky? I guess luck was all it was, because all my girlfriends were always talking about not being able to meet someone nice, good-looking, smart, and with a big dick, even an average-size one would do on an average man. They all kept asking me, "Where is he?" They said that all the men they had dated had dicks so tiny it would be a sin to sleep with them because they were the ones who had to look at that tiny pitiful little thing down there every day, bless their hearts! In my mind, I'm smiling and thinking, "Honey, the best one so far is standing right in front of my silly smiling face, and I couldn't be any happier than at this moment, at this time in my up-until-now dull life here in Fairhope." This horse was going to rock my world, and every chance I got. God knows I was ready; it had been far too long with no sex at all. It had been six long months waiting to see if this was the man for me or not. After that night, we made love every night and twice a night on the weekends! It felt good to be in my old routine again. I was tuned in to his body, mind, and spirit, as he was tuned in to mine, and we were both falling in love with each other. We turned out to be a perfect fit for each other in every way. Finally, at the age of forty-two, I had found the right man for me and that dream of living happily ever after might come true after all. Time would tell.

Rich rented a cute little house on Mobile Bay in downtown Fairhope, and we had one of the best summers either of us had ever had living on the water. We would take a lot of moonlight swims in the bay, in the nude, which I always loved doing. We played golf, rode up over the Fairhope pier in a hot-air balloon, and went to several Mardi Gras balls in Fairhope and in Mobile. We worked out together by biking and lots of walking. At age forty-two, I was in the best physical shape of my life, and he liked looking at me all the time. I could not take my eyes off him either.

Everyone thought we made the perfect couple, especially when the boys were with us; best of all, I was falling in love with his two boys as much as I was falling in love with Rich. The boys seemed to be warming up to Miss Linnie, since it had been almost a year since I met them. I loved that they called me Miss Linnie. I also taught Rich how to give me a massage using my famous techniques, down to the last detail. When I would give him an hour massage, he would give me a two-hour massage. That was something no one else has ever done for me to this day. He was one of the smartest men I had ever met. He graduated at the top of his class at Auburn in pharmacy school. He didn't seem to mind that I never went to college and that I wasn't as smart as he was.

I guess it was because we had so much fun when we were together. I let him be himself, and maybe because we were making love every night and I let him kiss me anytime he wanted to, who knows? All I did know was that he loved me, and I loved him, and I wanted to marry him. I wanted to marry him so bad that I did something so stupid one summer night. I made us a really nice picnic basket of wine and cheese with the crystal glasses and all the trimmings, and we walked down to the bluff that overlooks the Fairhope pier. There is a park bench and a large dogwood tree next to it. I got so caught up in the romantic moment on May 27, I was about to explode for him to ask me to marry him, so I jumped the gun and asked him to marry me! How stupid I felt when he told me, in his own nice way, that he wasn't ready yet to jump back into another marriage this soon after his divorce. I just could not stop the words from coming out of my big fat mouth. Anyway, I respected his reason and got over his rejection pretty quick. What a moment it was though, with the full moon shining down on us, drinking lots of good wine, and then me and my big mouth asking the big question. Wow! I remember that night so well.

As time went on, though, it was good that I waited for him to ask me. We had a movie, *Under Siege*, being filmed in our area, and Steven Seagal and his movie crew were in town for five months.

My business was taking off for the better because I was getting more and more famous actors finding out about me being an LMT, and they wanted me to work on them. I worked on most of the cast and crew of *Under Siege* for the five months they were filming in Fairhope and Mobile. What a fun time that was for me and all of my friends, too. My friend Donna was my hairstylist and my best friend. I would take her with me when I would do mini-massages while they were filming at the USS *Alabama* and at our local airport. She would help me carry all of my equipment and set up. She loved seeing all the good-looking actors, and especially one actor who also got my attention. His name was John Laughlin, and he really liked me a lot and came to me every day for an hour massage, as a lot of the actors did. He was a really good actor and lived in West Hollywood. But most of all, he was so good-looking and smart, and we seemed to have made a connection with each other. Donna and I really loved talking to him and getting to know him better. Since Donna was single, when John finally asked me out, I told him I could not go because I was dating Rich, but he could ask Donna because she would love to go out with him. Well, he took Donna out and the next day she called me bright and early to tell me I made a huge mistake for not going out with him. When I asked her what happened and why it was such a big mistake, she screamed out, "Oh my God, it was the best sex I had ever had and dinner at the Grand Hotel was good, too!" I told her I was going to kill her for having so much damn fun, and tell me all about it. She said he had the biggest dick she had ever seen, and the sex was so damn good that she was ruined for life to even look at another man. I told myself again if I had gone out with him and had sex with him and a good dinner at the Grand Hotel, I would have again been with another beautiful well-endowed man in my Forrest Gump life of being in the right place at the right time. How can that be, and now I am now forty-five years old? I had to keep telling myself that I was glad I didn't go out with him and glad that Donna had the time of her life. But how stupid I was to pass him up when Rich and I weren't even engaged yet. What the hell was I thinking to tell him no? It probably just would have been that one time and one time only, and he would have been on his way back to Hollywood. I would have never seen him again.

The next few days went by, and John Laughlin was so hell-bent on wanting me to go out with him so bad he even sent me roses, and I still said no. Sending me the roses really pissed Rich off, but I thought it was so sweet for him to go to that effort. I think John liked the fact that he just wanted someone he knew he couldn't have. As nice, smart, and good-looking as he was—and caring around that beautiful dick he was packing—I bet I was the only woman in his life who ever rejected him! I was trying hard to be the true Southern lady I had turned into again because of Rich and his boys. I asked myself, *Am I just being loyal or in this case being stupid?* Anyway, John Laughlin will always have a special place in my heart, and even now I wish I could see him again to say, "Hey, I made a huge mistake back then, give me another chance. I should have gone out with you!" He and Donna only had that one night, and she never heard from him again. When he left Fairhope five months later, he and I remained the best of friends for years and I even wrote to him several times. Little did I realize that our paths would cross again years later.

To my complete surprise, in the winter of 1993, when I did not see it coming, Rich finally asked me to marry him. It was one of the happiest days of my life and his too! He took me to dinner at one of the nicest places in Mobile named the Pillars, and when he got down on one knee, took my hand, and asked me to spend the rest of my life with him and his two boys, I couldn't stop smiling and crying tears of happiness all at the same time! I had waited a lifetime, it seemed, for this day to come, and I was ready and willing to be the best wife and mother to his two boys that I could be. I would love every moment of being married again for the third and, I prayed, the final time. Rich had not only brought lots of happiness into my lonely life, but he brought my faith in God back into my life.

We both had become active members of the United Methodist Church, and Rich was a spokesman for our church when the pastor was out of town. He made me so proud of him in more ways than I had experienced with any other husbands or lovers. I always wanted to have a husband who was a real Christian and someone who loved being involved with the church activities. My motto was, if you pray together you stay together. Being a part of our church family was very important to me. We never missed a Sunday or Wednesday night service, and we took the boys with us as often as we could. I had forgotten how important God was for any relationship, and after having lost Him for so many years, it was a joy to have Him back in my life again. My goals and values were finally on the right track again, and it was all because of Rich helping me find my way into the light after so many years of being in the darkness without God leading my way. Now I loved the light leading me down the right path of life of being a Christian lady again. Mama and Dad told me that was the best gift to them that they could ever receive, because I finally had God leading my way. They were thrilled about our marriage, but even more excited about me finding God again.

Rich and I spent quality time not only with our church friends but with some of the twelve or so close friends that we went sailing with every Thursday afternoon on a forty-two-foot sailboat at the Fairhope Yacht Club that our friend John owned. We loved how relaxed sailing made us both feel, and the sound of the water was music to our ears. We went to church on Wednesday nights and sailing on Thursday nights. I was in the church choir and loved music, so we even found time to go dancing at our favorite dance club in Mobile called Chantilly's, where Benny the Candy Man and I used to go dancing. I was praying that just once we would run into Benny and his wife, Diane, so he could see how happy I was with Rich. Some people even called him my boy toy because of our age difference. But I didn't care what they called us because I was in love and wanted the whole world to know how happy I was. I was proud to show off my boy toy every chance I had. With Fairhope being such a small town, I knew people were talking about us behind our backs, but the hell with them because I finally had the man of my dreams and soon to be the husband of my dreams. The way I look at people who love to gossip and aren't paying my bills is, the hell with them—they aren't my real friends anyway. Life was good, and I loved and cherished every moment we were together, and Rich did too.

On November 6, 1994, we were married at the Methodist Church, and for what I prayed would be the last time, Rodney walked me down the aisle. I prayed that God would bless our marriage. Our wedding was the most beautiful wedding I had ever had so far. We had all of my family there and his, too. The two boys, now age six, were also in the wedding as ring bearers. They too were so happy that Miss Linnie was going to be their new stepmom.

After so many years of being alone and searching for my perfect soul mate, I was so happy that this day had finally come. I had been single for eleven long years, so I was ready to jump into this marriage with both feet, and he was too. We had dated for almost four years, and I figured that I knew everything about him I needed to know and wanted to know. Even my OCD didn't seem to matter because I think he had a small case of it too. He tried to be so perfect and so organized in every way and with everything he did. I didn't have to worry about cleaning up after him. He even kept our garage spotless; dirty garages had always been a pet peeve of mine, and his too. I loved that because the garage is the first thing a person sees when they walk in your back door. To me, the way people keep up their home, cars, and garage is a reflection of who they really are. I loved that he liked to cook, clean, decorate, and take care of his two boys. He also loved making me happy, not just from having sex every day, but he was my eyes when I couldn't see, my ears when I couldn't hear, and my heart that made me come alive and truly beat again next to his.

I felt like we were the only two people in the world sometimes because we were so much in love. This feeling had not existed since Donnie and I were married many years ago, and it felt good again to experience this feeling that he completed me. I thought in my heart and in my soul that I was finally doing the right thing in my life with the right person who was the perfect fit for me. The ultimate moment came during the exchanging of our wedding vows. As we were looking into each other's eyes, we both saw into our souls through our eyes. We both truly saw our reflection of each other in our actual eyeballs. It was like no other experience I have ever had or probably will ever have again. It was a once-in-a-lifetime moment, and we both felt it at the same time in the same place, and it happened to be during the exchanging of our wedding vows on our wedding day. When we were walking down the aisle after it was over, we looked at each other, and I said, "Did you see what I saw through our eyes?" When he expressed the exact same emotion I did, it was like a sign that this marriage was meant to be, and God had blessed us with this sign from Him. From that moment on, we were ready for anything; I was so much in love with my new husband, and he was truly in love with me. I prayed that Rodney and the rest of my family and his family were as thrilled as we and his two boys were.

We had our reception in the church fellowship hall, and then afterward everyone came to the new custom home we had just built in Quail Creek. Our home was so big and beautiful, and although I did not want to sell my little pink house in downtown Fairhope, he made me, so I did. I wanted to rent it out, but I also needed the money, or at least part of it to build a treatment room over our garage at our new house. I hoped that since I was going to work out of our home and bring in some money for us, he would offer to build the treatment room for me, but he didn't. I only needed five thousand dollars. He was and always will be tight with the purse strings, but I mean that in a nice way, of course. When we did add the treatment room and a full bath and my office area, it turned out beautifully thanks to me selling my charming little cottage. We also had a covered, screened porch with a huge hot tub, which was nice for us and my clients. It was the first time in my life I had a brand-new home built from the ground up, custom built for us with all of our traditional touches in it everywhere. We even had Surround Sound in every room, which in 1994 was an amenity not many homes had at that time. Rich did a lot of the work himself. He was such a pretty boy, I would have never imagined that he would be the perfect handyman who could do it all and get his hands dirty, too! I helped him paint and do some smaller things in order to have the house ready in time for our wedding reception.

The timing was perfect, and we had every box put up and every picture hung before we entertained friends and family. He was as picky as I was about decorating. I found that to be a good thing because it took both of us to complete the job—it was such a huge house. We were turning it into a warm cozy home together, working as a team. I had never been that lucky with my other two husbands. They both loved the way I decorated and let me have the freedom to decorate our home any way I wanted to. With Rich, it was all about decorating our home and having fun doing it along the way. I thought to myself, *That sure does feel a little gay*, but as long as we were having sex, it was okay!

For our honeymoon, he planned to take me to London and Paris for two weeks after our wedding. We both were so excited about going to Europe. It was my second time abroad and his first. I got to thinking about what Major Ferguson had told me about calling him if we ever got to London, so I called. The major was glad to hear about me finally marrying my boy toy, as he had named Rich years earlier. I told him our schedule, and the major said that he would meet us at the airport when we arrived and take us on a tour of London, his way! When I asked him what way was that, he replied, "First class, of course."

When I told Rich what the major said, he replied, "I will believe it when I see it."

He had not known the major as long as I had. He thought the major was full of himself. I trusted that what the major said, he was going to do. I also knew that he was a man of his word; if he said that he would be there to pick us up, I believed him. To Rich's surprise, the major was indeed there, and he was even on time! Believe it or not, it turned out to be another Forrest Gump moment. He picked us up in his BMW station wagon and drove like a wild man, going too fast for my comfort level, but I told myself, *The hell with it. Off we go for a ride of a lifetime.* It turned out to be just that. He first took us to Buckingham Palace where Sarah (his daughter) had two rooms for her office area because at that time she was still married to Prince Andrew. Then we went out to eat at a place called Wheeler's, where he said that we were sitting in the queen's booth, although I couldn't see her there eating fish and chips like we were. It was his treat. Then he took us to our hotel, where he left us with a signed copy of his book, *The Galloping Major: My Life in Singular Times.* The date was November 8, 1994. When he told us good-bye, I had no idea it would be the last time I would ever see the famous Major Ronald Ferguson and my dearest friend alive. He died a few years later in 2003 at age 71 from prostate cancer, and I cherish the wonderful memories of him and of our trip to London with the best tour guide I could have ever wished for. What a way to start our honeymoon!

Rich was blown away by the whole thing, and we both went on with our tour of London by seeing the Tower of London and the queen's jewels.

We ate at some of the places the major recommended and took in some of the nightlife, which was a far cry from the nightlife in Fairhope, Alabama, to say the least. I got to thinking, *Mama, if you could see your blue baby now.* We were having the time of our lives and loving every minute of our new life as husband and wife. The second night we were there, we made the mistake of going into a huge nightclub that turned out to be a gay nightclub. The club was so big and the music was so loud that when I turned around to say something to Rich and check my coat, he was gone. We had become separated in the large mass of people, and I couldn't find him for over two hours. When we finally found each other outside the club, he said that he had been looking everywhere for me. When he lost me, he was so worried that we were never going to find each other again due to the huge mass of people. I told him the same story because I checked my coat, turned around, and Rich was gone. I was worried that someone had kidnapped him. He said that he had the same thoughts run through his head because the club was so big and the crowd was so wild. It was huge, bigger than our Walmart at home in Alabama. After we found each other, we left to go back to our hotel and said the hell with going dancing. We both agreed that if that happened again and we get lost, we should have a meeting place. Back in 1994 we had no cell phones like we have today, and I sure wish I had one that night more than ever.

The trip went on as planned, and we went on to Paris a few days later. The hotel we stayed in was near all the places we wanted to see, especially the Eiffel Tower, where at sunset we went to the top and watched the lights in Paris come to life. It was by far one of the most romantic moments we had experienced, and it was beautiful. We saw all the wonders that Paris had to offer, and to top it all off like a cherry on a sundae, Rich knew how to speak French to his new bride! I had no idea he was so fluent in French, and did it ever turn me on! All he had to do was say a couple of words, and I was all over him like monkey on a stick. He milked it the whole time we were in Paris, and I loved it.

We loved to dance and did find a couple of large dance clubs where there were straight people, and that was a lot of fun. We even rode a train to the south of France and saw the romantic countryside, which was a different kind of beauty than Paris. We also took a tour of Versailles while on our trip. It was in the winter, so we stayed warm by snuggling with each other every chance we got in and out of our hotel room. We ended up not acting like tourists at all, but more like the locals by dressing in black with lots of leather. Rich and I both had always had a weakness for leather, even in Fairhope. We both wished we could live and work in Europe because we loved the way Paris made us feel. It was almost like wearing the leather brought out the sexy, playful side of us, just like we were young kids again. We both felt so alive, and we were full of raw sexual energy.

We had made up our minds that when we got back to Fairhope, we were going to get rid of all our bright-colored clothes and all my little matching sundresses that looked so loud and bright. We wanted more tailored black coats, dresses, and suits. We had been bit by the Paris fashion bug. It felt good, and we looked damn good in all the clothes we had bought ... at least we thought we did. Rich and I also could not believe how loud we talked, always using our outside voice, until we went to Europe where they speak so nice and soft, always using their inside quiet voice. Me especially, using my horrible loud south Alabama hick voice that I have always hated. We made some new rules, and we were going to come back to the United States with a whole new European attitude and new clothes too.

When we returned from our trip, I couldn't wait to go over to Mom and Dad's house to tell them about our trip of a lifetime. As soon as I walked in the door, Mama said in her loud outside harsh voice, "What in the hell do you have on, and where in the hell do you think you are going to wear a get-up like that around here?"

All I could think of was, *Welcome back to the Redneck Riviera and good-bye to Linnie's World, for God's sake.* All I could say was "Thanks, Mama," using my south Alabama hick voice again that kicked in as soon as I walked in her door.

To this day, anytime she puts me down, that is the exact thing I say to her: "Thanks, Mama." She still rides my ass like a pony and never cuts me any slack whatsoever, wanting me to either be perfect all the time or just to see what kind of reaction she is going to get out of me. I have never figured out which to this day. I finally went back to wearing my cute Fairhope sundresses again because it is so damn hot down here on the Gulf Coast that we call the Redneck Riviera. I had to wear as little as possible to stay cool, but that's all right because I hated wearing clothes anyway any more than I had to. Just to test Mama sometimes and to see if she was still on top of her game, I would slip on a toe ring and tell my sisters to watch as I entered the room. Sure enough, she can spot a mole on a gnat's ass from a thousand yards away and say, "What in the hell is that on your toe?" Even if my hair, makeup, and outfit were perfect, I could get an ass-chewing most every day of my fun-filled life, but I'm used to it by now. Rodney tells me all the time Me-maw makes me a stronger person and keeps me on my toes. That's the way Mama is, and bless her heart, she will never change. That's all right, because I love her just like she is and always will be. We have fun picking at each other even to this day. At age eighty-five, she is at the top of her game and doesn't miss a thing when it comes to us girls.

Rich never liked Mama that much because when she would try to tell him what to do or what to wear, he would give her that "go to hell" look and tell her to mind her own business. No one had ever told Mama to mind her own business, and he went down as the first and last person to ever do that. God, I loved that man! He was my hero and also my husband until death do us part—or at least I thought that in Linnie's World!

About eight or nine months into our so-far perfect marriage, I could not put my finger on it, but Rich didn't seem to be giving our marriage his 100 percent effort as I was pouring my heart and soul into it each and every day. This time there was no way I was going to let my marriage fail. I was in it for better or worse, and I prayed he was, too. He kept telling me that the first year of marriage is always the worst for even the best of marriages, and again I trusted and believed everything he told me. Every marriage has ups and downs, hills and valleys, and right now we were stuck down in a deep valley.

I was so into him in every way, I just knew he was The One for me for the rest of my life. I kept telling myself that whatever it was, we could work it out. After all, when we took our vows at the altar, we both at the same time, through each other's blue eyes, saw the reflection of our hearts and souls. We had locked onto that moment of truth that no one could ever take away from us. There was only one thing that Rich had never told me, and it was five little words that I still hungered to hear: "Linnie, you are the one!" So far, I had not heard those five words out of his mouth, and it was okay because he told me over and over again that he loved me. Then I thought to myself that he acted like even those words were getting harder and harder to say to me.

What was going on with him? What was missing from our relationship, and when could I figure out what it was so I could fix it? When we made love every night, I felt that he was shouting as loud as he could that he loved me with his body and his heart. I always felt the love, but the words weren't there as often. When things were good, they were great. But when things were bad, they were very bad. The biggest mistake I could have ever made during our marriage was, after a heated argument, running home to Mama and Dad and telling them that we were having problems. That was not only a big mistake but a *huge* mistake, and I wish I could take it back and never do it again. It led to more and more serious problems at home between me and my husband. I should have worked it out with him and never said a word to anyone else.

Do not ever do that, because it will always come back to bite you in the ass every time. To this day, I could kick my ass for making that mistake. No matter who is right or wrong, your family will always take your side and make it easy for you to want to get out and say good-bye to someone who means the most in the world to you. Mama made it so easy for me with every marriage to pay them off and kick their ass out forever and never look back. She told me to learn from my mistakes. This time, I did not want to kick him out, because I loved my husband, and I loved his two boys and they loved me. They were my family now.

Mama and Dad both told me from the very beginning that something wasn't right with Rich. They just couldn't put their finger on it. I asked God to shine that light on me and keep me focused on getting my marriage back on track. I prayed hard to God for Him to give me a sign that things were going to get better for us. I needed my husband and my boys, and I loved them because they did complete me as the person I had become. Thanks to them, I had a purpose in life other than trying to be a good mom to Rodney every chance I got. That purpose seemed to be slipping further and further away each day.

Right before our first wedding anniversary, I thought that we both needed a break and needed to go somewhere that we both loved close to home. Rich and I loved New Orleans, and since it was only a couple hours away, it would be a perfect getaway for us. New Orleans was the perfect place, but as bad luck would have it for me, that weekend just happened to be the New Orleans Southern Decadence weekend in the French Quarter. It was as wild as you can get, with more good-looking gay men than I had ever seen in one spot at any one given time. It was considered to be the Mardi Gras day for all the gay people in the Southeast. Rich acted shocked at some of the sights, and so did I. Since that one time in London at the biggest gay club we had ever been to, of course by mistake, nothing really shocked us that much, but that weekend in New Orleans jumped to the top of the list.

Everywhere we went, nude men were walking around and dancing on the bars as we walked down Bourbon Street. It was like a train wreck; I couldn't stop looking at them, and neither could he. Rich would not hold my hand and acted more distant than ever to me … and then it hit me like a ton of bricks that my husband must be gay! Of all the places in the world to suggest going for a quiet getaway, I picked New Orleans Southern Decadence weekend. I threw myself under the bus and let it roll over me time and time again for making that stupid decision! Huge mistake, especially when we were already having some marriage problems to begin with.

When we got back to Fairhope, to our normal life, he confirmed it: "Yes, I know I am gay, and I have had it so far repressed deep down inside me that I can't live a lie any longer. That's why I am so mean and angry at times with you and my boys! I still love you, though, and I don't know what to do." As I held him in my arms, he let it all out and cried and cried. It was a tender side of Rich that I had never seen before.

He told me exactly what I feared to hear. My perfect life as I wanted it to be in Linnie's World was over. I felt more alone than ever. How was I going to deal with this situation? I loved him too! It brought back the horrible memories of when Donnie packed his things and left me years ago, except Donnie wasn't gay. I ask Rich what he was going to say to his two boys to explain to them that their dad was gay. All he said was that it was his business, and he would find a way when his boys get older.

So much anger and hostility was pouring out of the man I thought I knew. I could never figure out if he was angry that I helped him come out of the closet, or angry that his secret was finally going to be exposed after a lifetime of hiding it. He had turned into the biggest asshole I had ever seen, and the man I married was gone forever. My life with my husband and two little boys was over. What was I supposed to do now? The million little pieces began to finally fall into place. He told me that for years he'd had these feelings that he could not explain, ever since he was a little boy. He felt like men always looked at him in a strange way that he could never explain. He said that he felt uncomfortable being around good-looking men because he caught himself looking at them in a lustful way.

My son, Rodney, had just come out to me at the end of his senior year at Auburn. I found out within a three-month period of time that both my son and my husband were gay! But having been through it with Rodney, I could better understand what Rich was telling me. Rodney said that he knew he was different ever since he could remember, as far back as four and five years old. I had always known that he wasn't your typical little all-American boy, but I thought he would outgrow some of his somewhat gay behavior. Loving my son unconditionally, when he finally shared with me that he was gay, I told him that in my heart I already knew he was gay. I also told him I would always love him and support him whether he was gay or straight; it didn't matter to me, just as long as he was happy with himself as the good person he was born to be. As an adult, he is a strong, hard-working, sincere gay man who I'm so proud to call my son. He is a good person with a happy soul and giving personality who lights up my life every day. When he walks into a room, he charms everyone with his quick wit and fun-loving personality.

After reading all the information I could get my hands on, I knew that when people are gay, they don't choose to be gay, they are born this way. I can't imagine parents telling their child, their own flesh and blood, that if you say you are gay I will not love you anymore and I will disown you. I can't imagine parents telling their child that you have to make the decision and tell yourself to be straight again. A lot of people who call themselves Christians, if they are confronted with the subject of gay people, will always come back at you saying it's in the Bible that if you are gay you will go straight to hell. I also did extensive research to find out what the Bible has to say about homosexuals. In Leviticus 20:13 it says, "If a man lies with a male as with a woman, both of them shall be put to death for their abominable [which means causing abhorrence or hatred] deed; they have forfeited their lives." That means they will be put to death. I also found these rules about others being put to death for things that in our present day would be considered out of the question! Exodus 21:15: "Whoever strikes his father or mother shall be put to death." In the book of Leviticus 20:10: "If a man commits adultery with another man's wife, both the man and the woman must be put to death." Also in Leviticus 20:9: "All who curse their father or mother must be put to death. They are guilty of a capital offense."

I didn't realize the act of murder was rampant in the Holy Bible, especially in the Old Testament. I was shocked that there were so many laws that God had commanded people to be killed for all the reasons listed above, plus over fifty more verses that were written about killing people for all kinds of things they did wrong in the eyes of God. Back then, it was a common thing to do (kill people who went against God's rules), and a way of life for them to obey. Stop and think how many of us would have been dead before we even became adults if these rules still applied to us today and we did not obey the rules set for us in the Bible. They went by the laws and the rules of God or else they were put to death. In our present-day world, these laws and rules written thousands of years ago seem so foolish and not real in today's world. For God's sake, we would all be dead!

It is hard to see how these rules could be applied in our present-day way of life. All of this newfound information made me feel better that even if it is in our Holy Bible and you believe in Jesus Christ, people can and will continue to interpret the Bible in their own way.

I believe in our Lord Jesus Christ and God, and I feel like if Jesus was here with us on this earth right now in this present day, He would want all of His children to accept one another and love them for who they are as human beings. He would in no way say to people that He thought were not as perfect as Him that he could not love and accept them for who they are as people, gay or straight, black or white! I also want to believe that all people one day can open their minds and hearts to accept others for who they are and not label them or discriminate against them. I pray that they would keep an open mind to the fact that in our present day and time, there are scientific facts that prove people are born gay. For God's sake, it was on *Oprah*! Why would I question my son and now my husband, because why would they choose to be hated by the general public who are so ignorant and don't know all the facts of why gay people are born gay?

Some people I know who go to church every time the door opens and call themselves Christians, they detest the word "homosexual" when they hear someone say the word—much less consider that gay people are human beings like they are. These people who call themselves Christians have such hate in their hearts and no compassion for anyone who is gay whatsoever. These people are afraid to open their minds up and step out of their comfort level to get to know how wonderful, kind, talented, smart, and caring gay people really are. Accept them for who they really are, just like Jesus would want us to do in the present day. It could be your own child or grandchild who might be afraid to come out. Ask yourself if you would love your child any less, and if you have God's love in your heart as a real Christian. If you are a good loving parent, and in my case also a loving wife and mother, your love would be there no matter what.

So yes, I believe my son and my husband with all my heart that if they both say they are gay and they both know they were born that way and there is scientific proof of it, why would I ever doubt either one of them? If people are true to themselves, they know better than anyone; it's just that some gay people aren't strong enough to actually live a gay life. It is much too hard for them. They go through life like Rich and I, trying to be the perfect couple because that's what they consider normal to be. I wish I knew, what in the hell is "normal," anyway?

The movie and the book *Prayers for Bobby* comes to mind; it's a must-see movie. Take the time to read the book by Leroy Aarons as told by Bobby's mother, Mary Griffith. Read this book if you think or know for sure that you are gay or someone you know might be gay—read the book and, better yet, watch the movie. It will be an eye-opener to your heart and soul! It was to mine.

Believe it or not, I did understand and knew no matter how much I loved this man, my husband, Rich, the best thing I could do and the best gift I could give him was the gift of freedom—a divorce—so he could be himself. I could not picture my life without him and his boys. They were like the kids I had always wanted. I loved being his wife and the part-time mom to his kids. I loved them more than words could say, and I had no way to fight back to keep them.

My worst nightmare had come true, and I had another failed marriage. How could I face my family, my friends, and my life? Rodney even told me the first time he met Rich that he was gay. I should have listened to him and not listened to the lust and desire and what my body needed to feel like a woman again. I even thought Rich was gay the first time I laid eyes on him. I keep asking myself, why didn't I go with my gut feeling and listen to that voice inside of me telling me that he might be gay when all of the signs were there right in front of me? I wanted to believe otherwise because he seemed too good to be true. How could I face our church family? Most of all, how could I face Mama and Dad and tell them they were right all along? They thought that he was gay a year earlier when he was building our new home. He had all these ideas of decorating it his way. They knew then but didn't say anything because they knew he would sooner or later come out of the closet.

I loved him so much. Being true to myself, I knew he was gay, but I kept blinders on, not really wanting to know if he was or not. I didn't want that wonderful feeling of happiness I had with him to ever leave me. I loved being married again, and being a good wife and a good mom to his boys meant everything to me. I was hoping it wasn't true and wishing my life with him could go back to what it was and we could stay married, even if he was gay. I knew the reality of it was more than I could take, and I truly didn't know what to do but cry.

After months of tears and soul-searching, I knew that life had to go on. I had to move out of our beautiful new home that he had built for us and start over once again. I had sold my cute little pink house in downtown Fairhope and had no place to go. I told myself I couldn't stay in this small town of Fairhope with all these people talking about us. I really cared back then; now, at sixty years old, I don't give a damn.

I decided to move to a place where it was fun all the time and people didn't care or give a damn about who or what you were. Since New Orleans was only two-and-a-half hours from Fairhope, I decided to move there and get a job. In New Orleans, I would never be lonely again. I would leave my so-called normal life and move where every day was a party and it was anything but normal. Rich was the one who should have moved to New Orleans, not me! He even talked about it, but due to his good job in Fairhope and not wanting to leave his boys, he couldn't move away. From as far back as I could remember, I had always wanted to live in the French Quarter. Now was as good a time as ever to do it!

Rich and I divorced after five wonderful years together and only one year of marriage. I will always love him, and I will always love his two boys and cherish the memories of our wonderful life together. I had willingly given up what I had searched a lifetime for and lost the man of my dreams. I lost the second love of my life (as of that time in my life), and the hurt in my heart was like a knife had been stuck in it once again. I loved Rich so much that I knew I had to let him go so that he could be happy. He could be who he was born to be. How was I going to be happy again? Where would I find happiness when all I wanted was my husband and my family back? I was sick for months and could not sleep or stop crying. I tried and tried to pull myself together in order to function enough to find a place to live and a job. Now I had no husband, no home, no job, and no hope of ever being happy again. I had hit rock bottom again. I could not shake it off as easily as I wanted to. I knew it would take me years to find closure.

My luck was about to change. I found a charming one-bedroom apartment in the French Quarter of New Orleans. I also found a job as the in-house massage therapist for the Inter- Continental Hotel on Royal Street. New Orleans was looking better and better to me, and I was on the road to healing my broken heart. I wanted to keep the man of my dreams, but the reality was he was gay, he was born gay, and he will always be gay—married or not. I had everything except a straight husband, and it was not fair to him for me not to set him free. I had to keep convincing myself that I did the right thing by setting him free, and I had to do what I did for both of us.

He had even written me the most heartfelt letter after I moved to New Orleans, wanting me to come back to him. He asked me to please come back to our beautiful home and the wonderful life we had together with our two boys. He wrote that they missed me too, more than words could say. I still let him go. To this day, I wonder sometimes what would have happened if I had gone back to our life together and if that would have made us both happy, and for how long?

My heart kept telling me to go back to Fairhope and keep living a lie, because we were happy together as a married couple. But my good common sense won out. I lost everything in return—my family, my soul mate, the best lover I ever had, my home, and my business—and was left with this empty feeling of loss that I wasn't sure would ever leave me. I wondered if I would ever find anyone else who made me feel like a good woman and a good wife as much as he made me feel. I wondered if I would ever feel happy and laugh again.

Time would tell, but first I had to get to know who Linnie was and be happy with her as a person starting over yet again and now much older, on her own again. I had my work cut out, and my new best friends, Adam and Lee, also had their work cut out to keep me entertained and most of all help me laugh again. What better place to laugh and have fun but the fun capital of the deep South, the Big Easy, New Orleans, my favorite city in the world?

Chapter 7

MOVING TO NEW ORLEANS
AND STARTING OVER AGAIN

Leaving one of the safest places in the United States—Fairhope, Alabama—and moving to the wildest, most unsafe place—New Orleans—I was told by everyone I knew, including my son, Rodney, and my family, that I had really gone off the deep end and was completely crazy. I thought to my pitiful self, *That was a pretty off the chart crazy thing to do*, but yet in another way I was ready to move to a big city to see what it was like and if the city would like me.

I loved my quaint little one-bedroom apartment and took my time to get to know the gay neighborhood I had moved into. When I moved, I had no clue it was a gay neighborhood and found out after the moving van had already left me and my stuff there! But I found out a gay neighborhood was the safest place to live in the French Quarter—and the cleanest, too. Although being the cleanest was a far stretch from Fairhope and how clean it was, where you never even saw a gum wrapper on the ground. I had to keep telling myself that I had to move on and remember, *Linnie, you are not in Fairhope anymore.* I also kept telling myself to get over it and stop crying like a pussy because I was a big-city girl now. I was hell-bent on

121

telling my crazy self that I did the right thing by moving away and giving my husband his freedom.

I loved being able to walk everywhere; even walking to work every day was an adventure that I looked forward to. If I got bored or homesick missing Rodney, Mama, and Dad, all I had to do was walk out of my front door and watch the show that went on 24-7, and what a show it was! From the tourists to the local drag queens to the local shop owners, everyone was looking at everyone but could not care less what any of them were doing or give a damn who they were doing it with. In Fairhope, everyone was trying to find out all about your personal business just to have something to talk about. In New Orleans no one cared, and people were free to be who they really were—gay, straight, black, white, it did not matter. I loved that about my new city that I now called home, the Big Easy. I lived across the street from Good Friends Bar; I had to learn how to sleep with earplugs because it got so loud all the time, day or night. I lived one street over from Bourbon Street on Dauphine Street, and that too was loud, but what fun I had seeing all the colorful people and the wonderful music. I was having so much fun and was never bored.

It was a big deal finding a parking spot for my car. They will tow you, and God only knows where they take your car. If you were parked on the wrong street when the street sweepers cleaned the streets, you were towed. If you parked anywhere near a yellow line, you were towed. If you didn't have a parking pass for living in the French Quarter, you were given a ticket. Every now and then, I would see my good friend and longtime client Kenny McLean, a polo player from Point Clear, Alabama. He was doing exactly what I was doing, driving around the quarter looking for a good parking spot. He and his wife kept an apartment in the French Quarter to use on weekends. We usually would just let out a good ol' loud Alabama yell of "Hey, how ya doing?" and continue our search for the perfect parking spot.

I worked at the InterContinental hotel in the Classic Concepts Salon/Spa, and my two new best friends were Adam, who owned the shop and was a hairstylist, and Lee, who was also a hairstylist and a local drag queen. Of course they both were gay, eye candy to look at, and lots of fun. Most of all, they loved Miss Linnie from day one, and I loved them right back!

They were the two people who were trying their best to bring me out of my depression. We had fun from the time we opened the shop until we closed, and even then we would all go out after work for dinner and drinks. There was never a dull moment when they were around. Thanks to Adam and Lee, the tears from missing Rich finally went away, and I fell in love with both of them. They were my new best friends. They saved my life and made coming to work and living in the French Quarter an adventure every day. From one day to the next, I never knew what they were going to wear to work or what kind of drama happened to them the night before. The stories from the night before were the best and anything but dull. They held nothing back when they would tell me all the nasty details. God, I love those two old fools who made me love life again!

We had a built-in clientele from the hotel. We were busy most of the time, which meant I was making some serious money every day as the only in-house LMT.

I spent my time after work, a few days a month, dressing up in costumes that Adam designed. They were Mardi Gras costumes that we wore all during the year and not just during the Mardi Gras season. We worked with all the conventioneers who came to the hotels in the area. It seemed like every tourist who visited New Orleans thought that Mardi Gras was all year round. In reality, Mardi Gras was just the few weeks before Ash Wednesday each year. Adam took full advantage of them not knowing this, and so we would have special events all year to entertain the tourists who were mostly attending conventions and staying in town for a few days. The convention sales department of all the major hotels would hire Adam, and he would hire us. That was extra money for me, and I probably would have done it for free because it was so much fun. We had the outfits, lots of beads, feathers, and headdresses that Adam made by hand. We had a ball because we all wore masks that covered our faces. We could act like fools if we wanted to because no one knew who we were with our faces covered. That opened a whole new door to Linnie's World that had never been opened before! I could be anyone I wanted to be when I had on my beautiful outfit, feathers, and mask. Adam would dress me and Lee and hire several others to wear these beautiful, wild Mardi Gras outfits. He also did our hair—in wild, crazy updos—and our makeup. He used to work in Hollywood and was a master when it came to hair and makeup. He continues to work to this day with a number of motion-picture production companies and A-list actors.

Marching down Bourbon Street with our crazy band of misfits, I did not have to act like the prim and proper little Southern belle from Fairhope, Alabama, any longer, and I loved it. I could just be Linnie—let my hair down, relax, and be my silly crazy old self any time I wanted to. If I was dressed up like a slut on Bourbon Street in feathers with my mask on, I got into playing the part. We would dance and do our second line (famous dance step in New Orleans) down Royal Street with the famous Excelsior Brass Band leading us. The Excelsior Brass Band was the oldest marching band in New Orleans, dating back to 1879, and they were fabulous! Marching to the beat of the band, the conventioneers loved it as we led them through the French Quarter to the awaiting riverboat dinner cruise.

It was like being an actress, and I was born to play these parts whenever I had the chance. At that time, after my third divorce, I was still thin and a size eight with the tiny waist and always the big tits. I was looking good and feeling so sexy again in the clothes Adam made for me. To deal with the stress from the divorce, I could now afford a personal trainer to keep my five-foot-eight-inch body firm and in shape. Plus, I rode my bike to work every day feeling like the Wicked Witch of the West trying to dodge the taxicabs. Adam was like an artist, and Lee and I were his canvas when he would do our makeup and hair, no matter if we were going out to a bar or marching to the riverboats with the Excelsior Brass Band. I was getting spoiled by my new best friends and loved it!

Our very first function after I moved there was a White Party for the queen of England's birthday, and everyone had to dress in white. We left the ballroom at the Royal Sonesta Hotel and marched through the French Quarter all the way to the riverboat on the Mississippi River, where we had dinner on the riverboat named the *Delta Queen*. The cool weather was perfect, and it was a fun parade for everyone marching down Royal Street. During our ten-block march, everyone on the balconies threw white confetti. It was raining white throughout the quarter, and it was the most beautiful sight I had ever seen as the sunlight glowed off the white confetti.

Early that afternoon it had rained, but the rain had stopped and a rainbow had formed down at the end of the street so all you could see was the rainbow in back of the white confetti floating like snow. That sight was the most unique thing I had ever seen as yet in the French Quarter. We had a ball throughout the late evening thanks to the queen of England, but most of all thanks to my old queens, Lee and Adam. My life now was far from being dull thanks to all those fun queens and quirky colorful people! Adam and I fondly named Lee our "Old Fool" because he was the oldest of us three. They called me "The Princess," and of course Adam was the "Queen" who told Miss Linnie and the Old Fool what to do, and we did it.

There were so many movies filmed in the French Quarter that every time we turned around we saw movie stars. Now in Linnie's World, I felt like a movie star and one of New Orleans's famous hidden talents. I called my friend Claudia at the New Orleans Talent Agency who became my agent. I started getting parts as an extra in movies and television commercials. I was in several movies, including the movie with Ashley Judd named *Double Jeopardy*. I was in the rain scene with a hundred other extras with umbrellas. To this day, I have never been able to find myself in the movie, after watching it a hundred times. The extra income did not hurt either. Although it was not much, they did feed us well while we were on the movie sets. All we did was hurry up and wait. I found out that you needed to not be in any kind of hurry while filming a movie.

It passed the time for me on my days off and at night. It also kept my mind off missing my husband who was on my mind a lot, especially at night. My body missed him as well, since I went from having sex every night for over five years to zero sex now. Rich loved the rule that I was comfortable with having sex every night. He always told me, "If you see Donnie, thank him for me!" I saw several good-looking men, but none who I wanted to have sex with this soon after my divorce. I was hoping time would heal that part of my life as well. Adam and Lee kept pushing me to go on dates with some of the actors I had made friends with on the movie sets. None of them came close to the chemistry I had with my long lost love, actor John Laughlin, who I was so sexually drawn to like a magnet. But I gave him up to my friend Donna like a fool because I was dating Rich at the time. I could still kick my ass for doing that. Donna is still thanking me for the best sex she has ever had. *If I could just have another chance with him,* I kept telling myself, *I sure would not blow it again.* As time went on, I got more and more used to being single again and comfortable being alone. It was my choice, and living in the heart of the French Quarter, I really wasn't ever alone—all I had to do was walk out my front door and surprise, it was always showtime in one way or another. It made life fun each day and far from ever being dull. It was a world away from my roots in Fairhope, although I could be there on the weekend to visit my mom and dad in just a little over two hours. They still could not believe that I would ever dare to leave the safest and cleanest place in the South, which was Fairhope, Alabama, and move to the heart of the most dangerous and dirtiest place, New Orleans.

I never thought of it as anything but a great adventure for me to actually live in the most charming place I had ever seen, with the most colorful unique people I had ever met face to face. Just my walk to work each day was an eye opener, to see what I saw and of course smell the flavors of the French Quarter. I felt like that was where I was meant to be at that time in my uncertain life. I embraced it with open arms and of course my open mind as well. I was certain that this was my city, and I loved New Orleans as if I had been born and raised there.

I was actually looked upon as being one of the—few and far between— "normal" people living there. That was better than how I was looked upon living in Fairhope all my life, because I hardly ever fit the mold of the little prim and proper Methodist college graduate who not only had the proper education, but the matching purse to her cute little outfit every day. I was proud that I had a very successful business that proved itself for nine-and-a-half years in Fairhope. I was proud that I was the first LMT in Fairhope. I was proud that they named me Massage Therapist to the Stars. I would usually walk on the movie sets with no problem since I was carrying my high-touch massage chair to offer some mini-massages to the cast and crew. Some of the big A-list actors would make an appointment at the hotel so they could experience the hour-plus pampering package I offered.

My very first movie was *Lolita* starring Jeremy Irons. The movie production companies kept coming, and I kept going to greet them and welcome them to what I now called my wonderful city and my wonderful home, New Orleans. Because of my consistent job as the in-house massage therapist for the InterContinental hotel, the word was getting out to all the other large hotels about me being Massage Therapist to the Stars. They even wrote up a huge article in *Gambit* magazine, which was our local New Orleans publication.

I was so busy working on clients all day and sometimes late into the night that sex was actually, for the first time in my life, put on the back burner of my mind. It also had something to do with me being in my late forties and going through the change of life. Adam and Lee still kept on me to start dating and get out there with some straight people. The thing was, I did not know any straight people—all my friends were gay. All my life, I had always been drawn to people who were different and unusual like me. I have always been very different, to say the least, just like they were different in their own way. I was, after all, born a blue baby, and they were born gay, so we have a common bond for God's sake, and they were not going to get rid of Miss Linnie any time soon.

Now that I was living in New Orleans, I saw more Mardi Gras parades than I had ever seen before because of the convenience of the InterContinental's VIP viewing stands. They were set up every year in front of the hotel on Royal Street on the main parade route. I loved not having to get down on the street and get my knuckles skinned up trying to catch a moon pie or beads. I had the luxury of access to the VIP area if I wanted it to watch a parade. I was from Mobile, Alabama, the home and founding city of Mardi Gras. The city of New Orleans knew how to party and how to play it up in a bigger way than Mobile. Every night the city came alive with music and mayhem, and I was in the middle of all the action. I loved it.

One of the most memorable evenings I had living in the Big Easy happened when I least expected it. I went to an art show at the Hanson Gallery on Royal Street. It was a night that would change my life. I always loved going to these art shows because I always met the most wonderfully talented artists, and I too love to paint. Of course, all the colorful people who came were fun too. No matter how strange the art was or, especially, how strange the artists were, no one ever judged you, no matter what you were—rich or poor, black or white, happy or sad, ugly or good looking, it didn't matter. Everyone was treated equally, and everyone was out to have a good time and enjoy getting into the moment.

As I was taking in the art and all of the sights, I happened to glance across the room and saw a tall, dark, very good-looking man with beautiful black hair and brown eyes staring at me. He was either Spanish or Italian, and our eyes met for the first time. As he made his way across the room, I had to catch myself looking right at his crotch. He had on some tailored slacks that fit his tall athletic body to a tee. He looked like he was packing something big in his pocket, or else he was very glad to see me! Either way, his crotch had my complete attention. As he looked into my blue eyes, he said in his beautiful, low, sexy voice, "Hello. My name is Tony," and I thought to myself, *Of course it is!* We exchanged small talk, and I could not help thinking that he wasn't blond and didn't have blue eyes like all my other lovers did. I loved his soft sexy voice—and the way he looked like a model on the cover of *GQ Magazine*.

He was a local boy from New Orleans and seemed to be very well-educated. He was very interesting to talk to, but most of all he was straight, and he was interested in me. As the night went on, and it got later and later, and I had had several glasses of wine, I found myself extremely turned on by him. The only turn-off that held me back from wanting Tony to ask me out on a date was how his shoes looked. They were not polished, and were somewhat worn down on the heel and soles. You could tell that at one time they were expensive shoes. My dad taught me you can always judge a man or a woman by their shoes. How they take care of their shoes tells a lot about how they take care of themselves and how they would take care of you. Also, if my best friends Adam and Lee saw his shoes, I could hear them saying, "Nice outfit, but the shoes have got to go." They would have picked him apart from head to toe in less than two minutes. Since I was so taken by how tall and good-looking Tony was, I told my horny self, *The hell with the shoes, show me what's in your pocket.* Tony was the best eye candy I had seen since my divorce. I also loved the fact that Tony could speak Spanish. That alone was such a turn-on for me, just like when Rich spoke French to me while we were in Paris. I loved that! Tony also did not have any sign of a Southern accent or even a real New Orleans accent, and I loved that too. For some strange reason, since being married to Donnie, I never wanted to date or marry anyone who had a real Southern accent. My Southern hick accent was strong enough that I hated to hear my own voice because of it. Most people, though, loved my Southern accent, including my new best friend who I fondly named "Tony the Pony." He looked like a tall, good-looking Italian stallion.

I had my "Southern Lady Trick" that through the years had worked for me, and I was hoping it would work on Tony the Pony. The trick would keep me from having a one-night stand. I am proud to say I have never had a one-night stand, and now that I was pushing fifty, I did not want to break my perfect record. You ladies pay close attention to the details of how to accomplish the Southern Lady Trick that has never failed for me, and it won't fail for you either if you do it right! I acted like I was getting a little bit tipsy from the wine being served at the art show. As the time flew by, I still pretended I was tipsy (I really wasn't). I found a dark corner of the art gallery where we snuggled up sitting next to each other on a sofa. I was flirting and talking in my soft low sexy voice that is only heard by the person I want to have sex with. Tony was responding well, if you know what I mean. I slowly started to rub his upper thigh. I knew now was the time to slowly move my hand up and to the left and then to the right where I hit pay dirt on top of his tailored slacks. I was able to cop a feel—"accidentally," of course. My Southern Lady Trick *had* to look like it was an accident. Remember, I'm so shallow and obsessed with penis size and having the best eye candy I can find. I was pleased to report again that my spotless record had yet to be broken. Tony was not only six foot two, tall, dark, and handsome, but was packing about ten inches, maybe even bigger, between his long muscular legs.

To my complete surprise, though, Tony was a Southern gentleman, very shy and embarrassed, and it upset him that I would cop a feel when we hardly knew each other. But then, when he thought that I had too much to drink and that it was just an accident due to having too much to drink, that made it okay. In a man's mind, they are thinking to themselves, *Bless her heart, she's drunk and has no idea what she's doing. I wish she would grab it again when she is sober so she will remember how big it is!* Of course, I wasn't drunk and was fully aware of what I was doing. I was, all of a sudden, taken back myself to how could I be so lucky to meet such a nice, good-looking

Southern gentleman who had something I sure needed and wanted at the time. If Tony had not had such a nice surprise package between his legs when I took the liberty to cop a feel, I would have said that I was so sorry about that slip of my hand and said goodnight and it was nice to have met him. Remembering what my dad said about the worn shoes, I would have left the party empty-handed, more or less, if you know what I mean. Instead, I accepted a dinner invitation for the next night with Tony the Pony. Bad shoes or not, Miss Linnie needed to be laid. It had been almost ten months or more, and I needed sex *bad*. I needed "Tony the Ten-Inch Pony"!

Tony came to pick me up from work for our first date. I wanted him to meet my two best friends, Adam and Lee. It was like they were my daddy instead of my two best friends. They were protecting The Princess going out on her first date. I prayed to God Tony would not wear the same worn shoes, but he did. Just like Mama, Adam and Lee could spot a mole on a gnat's ass from a thousand yards away! They took one look at the shoes, rolled their eyes, and told me to come in the back room because we had to talk. The first thing they said was, "Oh my God, what's with the old ugly worn-out shoes?" Then, in a serious tone, they put their heads together and told me to do this: "Go out with him one time and have sex with him, and if the sex is good maybe two or three more times. Then girl, you better dump him and say good-bye." The same thoughts were in my mind too, but I didn't tell them that. I just had a gut feeling that said, *Don't forget the bad shoes*. I tried not to think about it, but it kept eating away at me no matter how much I wanted to have sex.

We ended up going out to eat at a wonderful restaurant on the lake in Metairie. Any place out of the French Quarter for me was too far away and out of my comfort zone. I enjoyed myself anyway because he knew New Orleans like the back of his hand. When we finished our meal and went to get back in his somewhat new car, the battery was dead. That should have been my second red flag or sign, other than the shoes, to run away and don't look back. He called his dad to come pick us up because they lived close by. On our very first date, I got to meet his mom and dad, and I thought they were a very attractive, nice couple. His mom looked just like Joan Collins, and his dad looked just like Anthony Quinn. They were the nicest, most normal people I had met so far living in New Orleans. They had a beautiful, big home in Metairie, and his mom had good taste in the way it was decorated. I was really impressed and could see that Tony had come from a good family and a nice home. They liked me from the moment they met me, and I liked them as well. When Tony took me back to my apartment in the quarter, we kissed and said goodnight. It was six or eight weeks of dating (no sex), because I wanted to get to know him as a friend first. I wanted to make sure that he might be The One before we had sex.

I finally got to see that big surprise package he had in his tailored slacks, and believe me, it was worth the wait! I was ten years older than him. I talk a big talk so much more than walk the walk, and I never have sex with a man until I get to know him first. I finally took that walk down the path of no return. At the time, all I was thinking about was just having sex and dating him every now and then, not actually wanting to marry him at all. Of course, Adam and Lee were telling me on a regular basis, "Bad shoes, bad boy, and bad idea. You need to dump him before you really start to fall for 'Tony the Italian Phony Hung Like a Ten-Inch Pony.'" The name really did fit, but the pony part was all I had my sordid mind on. I looked forward to riding that pretty Italian stallion as often as I could. If I knew then what I know now, I would have had a couple of good rides and said good-bye. That gut feeling was always in the back of my mind, reminding me of the worn shoes.

At the time I met him, Tony was a part-time actor and worked full-time at the power company as an electrical technician. He made an above-average income. He traveled out of town four days a week and was only home on the weekends. That was perfect for me, because I did not want someone who was up under me seven days a week. My busy schedule working at the hotel involved long, hard ten-hour days most all the time. That's why I was making good steady money. Tony was thinking that, since I had given up my apartment and had just bought a beautiful home right outside the French Quarter, I had a lot of money. The house that I planned to turn into a home had 4,200 square feet with a heated pool, hot tub attached, a beautiful waterfall, two fishponds, and a double lot that was gated with off-street parking. His thoughts were that this Southern lady who was ten years older than him could be his sugar mama. He thought from day one that I had a lot of money. If I could afford a house like that, I must be rich. I was, by far, anything but rich because I had purchased a money pit that was built in 1860. It needed lots and lots of renovation and tender loving care. I took the small amount of money I had left over from selling my home in Fairhope and put it into my charming old money pit to make it into my historic New Orleans dream home. I had all I could take with the noise and no parking in the French Quarter. It ended up eating my savings account up before I knew it, and the projects never ended as time went on.

I began to go into debt and needed a partner who could help me with my expenses on this money pit. The house had lots of charm like I had never experienced in my life. I had lived in a lot of places in lots of charming homes, but this was one-of-a-kind, so that made me work even harder to try to keep it up to my high standards of quality and appearance. That alone was a full-time job, but I was still young and had so much energy to work on this diamond in the rough.

All of my spare time and love went into this house, and I loved the results. It was called a raised Grand Victorian, and it lived up to its grand name in every way. It had 2,100 square feet upstairs on the main floor, with eighteen-foot ceilings and the original sixteen-foot Jefferson windows with the old original shutters that really would open and shut. The sixty-three-foot-long hallway and the half-circle dining room with six fourteen-inch-wide pillars in the main dining room with attached library overlooking the pool was as New Orleans as you could get. The downstairs was 2,100 square feet, and it had eight-foot ceilings, three full bedrooms with three full bathrooms, a huge living room, and nice big kitchen. The kitchen on the upper level was a gourmet kitchen with the highest quality Viking appliances and granite countertops. I guess if I had been Tony, I would have taken one look at this home and thought the same thing—this lady has lots of money. I'd always had good taste in decorating, and this home of mine was no exception. It was furnished with lots of antiques and furniture to fit the period of the house. That part of the renovation was the fun part to say the least, because I had always said that if I had not become a massage therapist, I would have become an interior decorator. I have always had an eye to bring it all together. It was also a good party house since I had the heated pool and built-in attached hot tub with a waterfall. The landscaping around the pool was also my idea, with lots of privacy and the feeling of being at a five-star spa resort. I had always wanted a place where I could swim nude anytime I wanted. That was possible with that pool and yard.

I found out very quickly that in New Orleans, when you own a home, you have to create your own security system. That was taken care of by me buying two new Doberman puppies, which I named Kraut and Kyra. My male, Kraut, grew up to be a sweet 110 pounds, and Kyra was at least 85 pounds and was not as sweet as her brother. They looked like real bad-ass guard dogs that could kill on command, but they were my babies. To say the least, no one was coming in or getting near the eight-foot iron gates that surrounded my property. The dogs made sure of that. Everyone in my neighborhood knew about Kraut and Kyra, and they of course told all of their friends and neighbors, so I felt safe all the time with my two babies at my side.

One day I overheard Tony on the phone when I was at his apartment out in Metairie saying, "Yes, Linnie and I are going to get married." That was the first and only time marriage had ever been brought up, and it wasn't me who brought it up. One of his old girlfriends who he had not heard from since we had started dating me wanted him to go out with her. After he told her that he was only dating me, he hung up the phone. I asked him why he told one of his old girlfriends that we were going to get married. All he could say was, "Well, why don't we get married?"

I was so taken aback by that piss-poor marriage proposal, I was speechless. I finally told him, after three husbands who made it a big deal to ask me to marry them, why in the hell would I marry anyone who proposed to me like that? The timing was piss-poor, too.

When I asked him if that was the way he was asking me to marry him, he said, "Yes."

I looked at him and said, "I am going to have to think about this, and I'll get back with you."

He was taken aback that I didn't say yes right away to a question that again would change my life for good. Right then and there, I told myself that I needed to leave his apartment and never come back.

Ms. Linnie Delmar

When I went to work the next day and told Adam and Lee about that piss-poor marriage proposal, they said that if I married "Tony the Phony," it would be the worst mistake I would ever make. They kept yelling at me to remember the bad shoes. I knew they were right, and I knew that I should listen to my inner spirit and that gut feeling that was also yelling out, *Do not marry this man.*

Since my divorce from Rich, I realized I had only been dating Tony because I was lonely and on the rebound, still sad from missing my husband Rich and the two boys. I kept thinking that maybe one day the three of them were going to come to New Orleans and pick me up just like Richard Gere did to Debra Winger in the movie *An Officer and a Gentleman.* I truly had that vision in my romantic mind. I thought any minute they would come through the door at work and take Miss Linnie back home to Fairhope, and we would live happily ever after. Of course that never happened, and they never came to get me. Being happy like that again was only in my dreams.

When Tony came along, at first it was just for the sex, but then when I got to know and love his wonderful mom and dad, I fell in love with them more than him. I wanted what they had, which was a loving family. I realize now that the hunger I had for a normal family to love and take care of was the idea in my mind, and I was in love with the idea more than the family life I wanted to have with Tony. I knew somewhere inside of me he could fulfill the empty places in my broken heart that I had from missing Rich and the boys. When I told Adam and Lee this, they said they already knew I was a dreamer, but brought up one fact that I kept trying to forget. It was the fact that Rich, my wonderful third husband, was gay for God's sake. I needed to get over it. They assured me that he was never going to walk through that door, pick my fat ass up in his arms, and take me back home to play house again. We were never going to live happily ever after. That nonsense was just in Linnie's World! I knew they were right, as usual, but my heart was still hurting from the loss, although I was trying to move on.

I knew by that gut feeling I was on the rebound, using Tony to pass the time and fill the gap in my broken heart. Tony did have his good points and had a lot of book sense and could pass any test on paper. He had also

134

been to college and was educated, but had very little common sense, if any. He was good to me, and the sex was good most of the time, but something about Tony was off. I could not put my finger on it. My mama and dad had only met him once or twice, and they too thought something was off, but like me they did not know what it was. When Rodney met him for the first time, he could not stand him and thought he was a stupid goof-off, and of course told me that to my face. It was not a complete surprise, though, because Rodney did not like most of the men I dated or married. He told me that I had poor taste in men. I should have paid attention to my son's good common sense, because his gut feeling was right 100 percent of the time.

An odd thing happened before Tony and I took the big step to get married. I got a phone call out of the blue one evening after work from my heartthrob actor friend John Laughlin from West Hollywood. He said that he was in New Orleans filming a movie and asked if I would like to meet him for a drink. I had been writing to him for years now in hopes that one day our paths would cross again. Today was that day. He did not have much time off from filming, and his schedule was tight. I could hear it in his voice that he wanted to see me.

I was at a restaurant with Tony and his entire family. We had at least ten people there for his sister's birthday. I received the call on my cell phone. I thought how rude it would be for me to leave all of them in the middle of dinner to go meet with another man who I had been dreaming of having sex with. God, it made me physically sick when I had to tell John I couldn't go, but I thanked him for the invite anyway. He was so surprised when I turned him down that he asked me in a sincere way, "How can you turn me down again? This will be the last time you will hear from me." Trying not to be so serious, I came back at him by telling him he could call Donna. As he began to laugh, he told me, "Like I told you the last time you turned me down, I don't want Donna, I want you!" My God, I wanted him too, but to my dismay, I made the biggest mistake in my life, and I could still kick my ass over not seeing that good-looking wonderful man when I had the chance. I never heard from him again. Last I heard, he had become a dad for the first time to a son, and he is probably married in Hollywood now to a beautiful model or actress. They probably lived happily ever after. I have seen him in so many movies and especially in some of the Danielle Steel miniseries on the Lifetime channel on television. Every time I see him, I think to my silly self that maybe in Linnie's World, we would have made the perfect couple and that he was my true soul mate all this time, but we just didn't know it yet. But most of all, how in the world could I have told him—not once but twice now—that I couldn't go out with him? Timing is everything, and our timing had been off both times he asked me out due to first Rich and now Tony. I guess it just wasn't meant to be for us to get together either time when he wanted me to go out with him.

After two weeks of waiting, Tony wanted and needed an answer to his question, "Will you marry me?" I was tired of feeling alone, and I needed help with my money-pit huge house. Although I had no clue who the real Tony was at the time, I loved his last name and thought it fit me to a tee. I also loved his family a lot and how well I seemed to fit into his family's way of life. I wanted a real family life again. That's the real reason I wanted to get married. I just wasn't sure if he was the right man for me, but I guessed time would tell. I prayed my son, Rodney, would do me the honor of walking me down the aisle one last time, and although he hated his soon-to-be stepdad, he said he would do it just for me. He said, "Mama, don't ever ask me again, because this will be the last time I do this for you." Now that I had a wedding to plan, my thoughts were clear and hopes were high that he just might turn out to be The One after all. Although I did not have the chemistry with Tony that I had with Donnie, Al, and Rich, I didn't want to live my life alone in the Big Easy anymore. I was ready to be married again. When I look back on my poor decision, all I can see is a very lonely lady named Linnie who just wanted to find a partner and a friend who would meet her halfway. I wanted us to work together as a team and to build a good life together as a family. I also know now that I should have just lived with him a while before I ever decided to get married again for the fourth time. My gut feeling told me over and over again to listen to my dad and remember, the way he takes care of his shoes is most likely the way he will take care of you!

Chapter 8

HUSBAND #4—TONY THE PONY

My 1860 Grand Victorian home was perfect for Tony to move into before our wedding. The renovation was complete, and the house couldn't have looked any better. He helped me complete all the projects that needed to be done before our wedding. All he owned was an antique dressing table, an old sofa, and his clothes—but most of all, let's not forget his worn shoes. The shoes were the first sign for me to get the hell out of Dodge like my dad, Adam, and Lee kept telling me: bad shoes, bad boy, bad idea. Dump him and run is what everyone told me to do, especially Rodney. I wasn't going to dump Tony the Pony; I was going to marry him instead. He was eye candy, and I was hoping there was more to him than just that shallow shell of a man.

He tried hard to bring home the bacon and take charge, but he had no common sense to do either. He was a strong man physically, but mentally he was weak in every way. I knew I would have to be the one who took charge and wore the pants in the family. It would be a first for me—my other husbands were smart and strong in every way (well, except for Merle the Pearl). I liked that they took charge and loved taking care of me. Tony was smart and had lots of book sense, but I would be the one making all the decisions for us when it came to doing anything major around the house because of his lack of common sense.

He did know his jazz and blues music, though. He knew the best local places to hear the best jazz and blues in the French Quarter. He was friends with most of the musicians in the city. He also knew the best local, small, quaint, hole-in-the-wall restaurants where we would eat out most every night. Since he was a local boy raised in New Orleans, he had several colorful people he called his close friends, like "J. Monkey Dee" and "Craig Jaming Jody" who wrote their own songs and performed on Bourbon Street every night.

Tony had not yet bought me an engagement ring, because he had no money. One day Adam and I were out window-shopping in the French Quarter and Adam saw the perfect wedding ring for me that we both loved. He was so against me marrying Tony that he could no longer speak to the man. I was his best friend, and he told me to go ahead and buy the wedding ring because it would be better than anything Tony would pick out. Plus, Tony had no money to get a ring of this quality, so I bought my own wedding ring. When I told Tony about it, he was thrilled. He loved the fact that he did not have to spend a dime, and I loved the ring. Adam told me later that one of the few things Tony had going for him was that he had no children and no baggage, and he was low-maintenance (reminding me again of the old worn-out shoes).

Everyone knew I was high-maintenance, and especially with me having OCD, I felt lucky that any man would have me on a full-time basis. Adam and Lee told me how foolish it was for me to think that of myself. They just loved me for me being me, and that thing about the OCD was just in Linnie's World of wanting things to be too organized and perfect all the time, nothing more and nothing less. Tony's parents were thrilled about our upcoming marriage. They purchased the most expensive wallpaper I had ever seen for our master bedroom on the upper level of my home. It was their wedding gift to us, and they couldn't be happier about welcoming their new daughter-in-law to their family. It was the best wedding gift we received. I couldn't have asked for better in-laws, because they were such good people. Knowing what I know now, I was taking the monkey off their backs. They knew I would take good care of their oldest son. Tony had some serious issues, but I truly felt like I could deal with anything that came along. I was going to make this marriage work no matter what, hell or high water. I was on a mission to live happily ever after with Tony the Pony. If only he would be willing to give our relationship a fifty-fifty chance, I was ready to try; that was my attitude, and failing the fourth time around wasn't an option for me.

On November 30, 1996, we were married at our home in New Orleans, and my son, Rodney, did walk me down the aisle. My dress was the same one I wore for marriage number three to Rich. I had bought my own ring—I could not afford a new wedding dress too. Plus I was still a perfect size eight. I looked damn good in this used designer wedding dress, wearing my new wedding ring that I bought for myself. By God, this was going to be a good wedding if it was the last thing I do! Rodney told me, "Mama, this is the very last time I am going to ever walk you down the aisle, and this time I mean it." Our wedding photos say it all—the look on my face and on Rodney's face, too. I looked like I was thinking, *What in the hell am I doing?* and Rodney's face seemed to say, *I hate this man so let's get it over with so I can get the hell out of here and go back to Atlanta as soon as possible.* The only people who looked totally happy were Tony and his parents, who looked great and were smiling from ear to ear. The reception was at our home, with a local band of misfits who played all drums and wore all white. As the drum band had more and more drinks, one girl (out of the fifteen or so members) started doing a belly dance and then stripping. That is when I knew it was a sign from God that we were not getting off to a good start on our wedding day. Plus, I busted Tony and "Craig Jaming Jody" smoking pot and high on pain pills on our wedding day. That was another sign from God, and it was not a good sign. I knew that Tony would smoke pot from time to time, but never in front of me. He knew how much I hated it and would not tolerate it when he drank too much.

I could not help but remember my wedding night with husband number two, Merle the Pearl. He was high as a kite off of Jack Daniels and Coke, and he too couldn't do it on our wedding night. All I could do was say to myself, *Linnie, you did it again, you made a huge mistake and now you have to suck it up and live with the fact that you aren't going to fail being married to this fuck-up of a new husband. It's not going to be easy, but you can do it. You have got to work hard to make this one work, even if it kills you and takes you to the poorhouse.* I asked myself if living happily ever after was just a fairy tale you only see in movies. I begged God to give me a sign, and then I thought of all the signs he had already given me that I ignored and all the red flags that went by the wayside. I was so stupid to not pay attention to something that would change my life forever. On my wedding day, I threw myself so far under the bus that I was black and blue for a month.

From my wedding day forward, just as we were settling into our newly married life and I thought things could not get any worse, they did. Less than two weeks later, Tony lost his job at the power company. I began to try to line up job interviews for him, but every interview he went to, he had an excuse of why they could not hire him. I would leave for work for my ten-hour-a-day job at the hotel every morning. I would have a list of odd jobs for him to help around the house while I was at work. When I got home, nothing had been done on the list, and I could clearly smell pot throughout the house that I had made into a beautiful home for us. Finally, when I couldn't take anymore, I told him to come with me because he was going to clean the pool, and he was going to do it in the nude. Even looking at my eye candy Tony the Pony got old real quick, and I got tired of being the only one trying to make this joke of a marriage work. I did everything I could to help him. I updated his portfolio so he could get more acting jobs. I even sent him to chef school because he said he thought he would make a good chef, even though I had never seen him cook a meal or boil water before. I did all of the cooking and cleaning. Most of all, though, I put him through rehab not once but twice to clean up his drug problem (hooked on pain pills), and I spent so much money on him. Finally, my insurance company would not pay for rehab any longer because he would check himself out saying he's off the pain pills forever. Of course, that was another lie, because within weeks he was right back on them.

After a very long four years of trying everything I could do to improve him, help him, and most of all heal him, nothing seemed to work because he wasn't willing to help himself. I was getting to my rope's end, and when I thought there wasn't anything else he could do that could hurt me or piss me off more than he already had, he did one more thing that I couldn't believe. I had just purchased a new computer, and I thought that he could find a job by learning how to use the computer. Instead of finding a job online, he mounted up over nine hundred dollars of charges on porn Web sites using my credit card. At this point, I had lost all hope and respect for him, and the last thing I wanted to do was make love to him. All of my respect for him was gone within the first year of our marriage.

His parents told me several times that they had tried to talk some sense into him to let him know he was on thin ice with me and one day I was going to say enough is enough and leave him. He once told me, as he looked into my blue eyes, that I liked looking at his good-looking body and huge dick so much I would never leave him. He said that he figured that out the first time (of many) that I made him clean the pool in the nude. The stupid shallow Linnie would pretend that he was my sexy pool boy! That's when I looked into my own eyes in the mirror and said to my sick self, *Who's the fool now for loving good-looking men with big dicks and attitudes to match?* He had used me for money, a free place to live for over four years, and taken full advantage of me. I had done everything to try to make this marriage work, but finally, through my eyes looking into my broken soul, I knew I was done and it was over.

Now how do I get out of this marriage and find a new start again? How do I get this monkey off *my* back? I had made such a mess of my life up to this point by picking the wrong man again, but I had to focus on what I needed to do to have any future ahead of me. I wanted to just call his parents and tell them to please come get him and keep him as far away from me as possible, but I knew it wasn't going to be that easy. I had kept him in a lifestyle that he loved and got used to, so he told me that he wasn't leaving unless I paid him off. He did not have to pay for anything for four years, and he wasn't going to start now. He told me that if I wanted a divorce, I would have to pay for it myself. I could see that signing the divorce papers and moving out was going to be another big problem I had to deal with. That just pissed me off even more, so I got serious about leaving his sorry ass. If I never see a big dick on a pretty boy again it will be too soon. I was so over Tony the Pony and wanted to leave him and leave New Orleans in order to get away from him.

When he was on pain pills, which was his drug of choice, he was as mean as a snake and would try to hurt me. He was so high on drugs he had no idea how strong he was, and he had no clue what he was doing when he was high. Toward the end, I had to call 911, and the police took him to jail. He was so mad at me when his dad got him out of jail that I did not feel safe at all being in the same room with him.

During this time, I still had to work and pay all of the bills in order to keep my home up. Finally, I could not do it anymore because I was out of money. I sold my beautiful home and had to move to another apartment with Tony. He would not leave because our divorce was not yet final. It wasn't until I paid him enough money to get out on his own that he finally left. That is when I decided to move to Atlanta to be near my son, Rodney, and get as far away from Tony as I could.

This was a move to Atlanta that I was looking forward to. Being single and alone was now looking better and better each day to me. What hurt me more than anything was to adopt out, give away, my two dogs, Kraut and Kyra. They were like my children. I found a good home for both of them, but my heart was broken as I said good-bye to my babies. They were my protectors for four years and did a good job because my home was never broke into nor did anyone come over my fence. I bought myself a very tiny Doberman who only weighed one pound, and I named her Coco Rochelle. To this day, she is the love of my life. She is now over six pounds but thinks she is a hundred and ten pounds like her brother Kraut, who she spent the first few months of her life with. She would even crawl up in his huge mouth and clean his teeth for him, and he never hurt her in any way. Coco was his baby, and she slept in his flank every night before I had to give him away. He was such a good dog, and I thought Tony might want him, but he could not take care of himself much less a big dog who required a lot of care.

Rodney came down from Atlanta to help me pack and so did my sister Val. They gave me moral support through this rough time that I was going through with Tony. Rodney was happy that I had finally seen the light of truth about what kind of person Tony was. He welcomed my decision to move to Atlanta. I was going to miss my wonderful job at the hotel. Most of all, I was going to miss my two old fools who were my best friends and family to me and Rodney, too. They knew why I had to move away, and of course they had to let me know one more time, "Miss Linnie, what did we tell you about bad shoes, bad boy, and bad idea. You should have dumped his ass a long time ago." All along, I knew they were right, but then we all had a weakness for eye candy and a well-endowed man. But now, I could honestly say I was over that too. From that day forward, I vowed to never again be the shallow shell of a woman who had to be with a boy toy who was eye candy. I needed to find out at age fifty who Linnie really was and why she had a pattern of always picking the wrong men who just so happened to be hung like a horse. I wasn't looking for that, it just happened to be that way with all four husbands, and look where that had gotten me now.

The city of New Orleans had been so good to me. I loved the old buildings, the music, the sounds of the French Quarter, and the good food. What I loved the most were the colorful people who loved life and accepted each other for who they were. I loved my job and getting to work with hotel guests I got to meet every day and working with more than ten motion-picture companies. I was an extra in the movies *Dracula 2000*, *Runaway Jury*, and *Double Vision*. I learned how to paint and use my talents through art, to express myself through my paintings. I loved all the Mardi Gras parades each and every year and looked forward to that time of year and all the madness that came with it. I will miss walking Coco through the French Quarter in her cute little outfits along the Mississippi River late in the evening. Having coffee and beignets at Café Du Monde with my friends and neighbors I had made living in the French Quarter. I will miss eating at all the famous and not-so-famous local restaurants in the quarter and loving the tastes and smells of it all. It was truly a life-changing six years that I will always cherish.

Even meeting Tony had its good times and cherished memories. I will truly miss his parents who loved me like family, and I loved them as well. Especially his only sister and her two wonderful girls, Ashley and Katie, who were like the daughters I never had. I will always remember the good times we had when his dad and mom took the whole family to Mexico and how beautiful it was in a country I had never been to. I have the artwork, two beautiful paintings, of the old hotel where we stayed and the old town we stayed in with all the flowers. I bought them to remind me of Puebla, Mexico, where Tony's dad was born. What a wonderful two weeks we spent together on vacation as one big happy family. I will remember the good times we had when Tony was off the pain pills. His soft, sexy voice when he spoke Spanish to me was music to my ears. I will miss his smell, his touch, the husband I wanted him to be, but he didn't want me as much as he wanted and needed the pain pills.

At least I knew—and he knew, too—that I did all I could to make it work. It just was not meant to be. God had given me all the signs once again, and I ignored them because I chose the eye candy instead of a real husband. I wanted a husband to love and respect and for him to love and respect me and want to take care of me instead of me taking care of him.

I also took with me some good stories that would stick with me forever anytime I even thought of taking another man in and being his caretaker, mommy, lover, housekeeper, much less his wife. Like the time I bought Tony the new, expensive pressure washer so that he could make some money on the side. He told me every day for four years that he was going to get a full-time job and never found one. I asked him one morning before I left for work to try the pressure washer out on our front porch to get the feel for it and learn how to use it properly. He told me it would not be a problem, because he already knew how to use a pressure washer. On the way to work it made me feel better knowing that he had some pressure-washing experience. All day at work, I couldn't wait to get home to find that he had cleaned not just the front porch, but the whole house, the pool area, and both fish ponds. Of course, wanting this dream to be a reality was only in Linnie's World.

Instead, when I returned home, the first thing I saw was that all the paint was missing from the front porch. Not just the paint, but the wood from the railings had been blown off, too. The house, after all, was like termites holding hands because it was so old. I not only saw all the damage, but when he blew the railings off the porch, he and the new pressure washer dropped fifteen feet below and he was laid out on the ground. No telling how long he had been there. I called 911 and off we went to the emergency room to see if he had any broken ribs. He did not have any broken bones because he was high as a kite from taking pain pills before he started pressure-washing. When he woke up in the hospital and came to his senses, he apologized for all the damage he had done. He said that he had no clue that the pressure washer was turned on wide open the whole time. Like I said before, the boy had no common sense whatsoever. The front porch cost me at least three months' salary because he had no salary to pay for it himself. I couldn't help but laugh to keep from crying, and I wondered how the boy lived this long to be forty years old?

The next story was just as funny and happened when he told me he wanted to go to chef school—so I sent him, of course, because our marriage was still new. I paid to send him to the best culinary school in the city of New Orleans. After the first day, he was all excited and told me he needed a new set of cutting knives for class the next day. Like a good mommy, I sent him to school with five hundred dollars to buy the knife set the school said he had to have. Every day he told me he thought he had found his new niche, and it was becoming a chef. This opportunity might be just was he was cut out to do, even more than acting. The acting jobs he sometimes would get were few and far between. But when he did get a job as an extra in a movie or television commercial, it paid well. I asked him one evening to show me how to cut up an onion and some okra so he could actually cook us something for supper. He began to cut using his new five-hundred-dollar knife set when he almost cut off his finger. I again had to take him to the emergency room for stitches, and of course he again needed lots of pain pills for the next few days. The chef school only lasted two days after he cut his finger; he was taking so many pain pills he could not stay awake in class, so they kicked him out. Just like a good wife, though, I again offered rehab and he accepted again, but in less than a week he checked himself out telling me he was cured and off the pills.

The story that I thought I would take to my grave was one to remember as well. It is so funny that I have to let everyone know, being in the right place at the right time was again another Forrest Gump moment in Linnie's World. A couple of years into our marriage, during a period when Tony was drug-free off the pain pills (or at least he convinced me he was), we took a Florida vacation. At that time in my career, I was making good money and could afford a first-class cruise we took out of Fort Lauderdale.

On the way down there, we were your typical tourists. We took in all the sites on the way down, and things were calm and pleasant with Tony and me. When we arrived at the beautiful ship and got to our room, I asked Tony in a calm voice if he noticed that everyone on board the ship had very little luggage. He of course did not notice or care. I thought he would be happy when I told him, "Surprise, we are about to take our first nude cruise together!"

He was speechless, and his olive skin turned completely white. After the shock, he began to yell out, "How dare you take me on a nude cruise and not tell me before we left New Orleans?"

I told him I wanted it to be a complete surprise, and oh buddy, it was!

After we got beyond international waters, they made the announcement that everyone could disrobe. We were still in our cabin. I tried to ease the tension and lie to him by telling him something I knew he always loved for me to say. I told him that since he was my handsome movie-star husband and my boy-toy eye candy, I wanted to show him to the world. He smiled and began to laugh. I knew this would be hard for him because he was shy, embarrassed because he always thought his dick was pretty but much too big to show off (that would be a dream come true for most men). He was also worried about what his family would think, due to the way he grew up in a Spanish household. I admired him for all those reasons, but now I was ready to go out of the door of our cabin and see what it was like being on a nude cruise. That was one of many items on my bucket list of things to do before I die. We opened the door and began walking down a long hallway with lights on that were far too bright for my comfort level. I had on my swimsuit with a cover-up holding my towel. Tony had on the tiny little swimsuit that I bought for him and his towel covering himself up as much as possible. The first two couples we passed along the way to the pool area were butt-ass naked, wearing only a smile and holding a towel. Our trip to the pool area had made it to the top of Linnie's World of wild and crazy things to do!

I have never had a problem going topless to a beach or anywhere, since I have always been told I have the perfect set of tits. I have been told this by every man I have ever been with. When you are told something like that your whole life, you begin to believe it, like being told you are a blue baby! I took off my top with no problem but taking off my bottoms was not going to happen, then or ever! I was the only woman poolside with clothes on. God forbid, I felt like everyone was looking at me. When I looked up, I found Tony had already stripped off butt-ass naked. He was sitting in a lounge chair so close to the pool that he could check out how cold the pool was with his dick. He had so much oil on that his perfect olive skin was glowing. He made sure that everyone could see how embarrassed he was.

After the second day of our five-day cruise, Tony was brown all over and his body was more beautiful than ever. I was totally burnt to a crisp, bright red color down to my bottoms, which were never coming off, sitting alone under an umbrella out of the sun. All the old people were staring at me and giving me that "go to hell" look I have seen before with clothes on. The average age was about forty-five to fifty and up (over 2,500 butt-ass old naked people). In Linnie's World, I thought, *That is not what I signed up for.* I was hoping that everyone was going to be my age and younger. Tony turned out to be the youngest man on the entire cruise, and of course the best-looking man as well. He was so comfortable now that when he fell asleep in the chair while sunning poolside, I had to make sure I sat next to him at all times. Every day a crowd of ladies and men would gather as close as they could to wherever we were sitting. It was like a train wreck they could not stop looking at. They could not take their eyes off the biggest dick they had ever seen. I had to keep that dangerous gun covered up to keep it from going off at any given time. Tony was feeling good, and he knew he was hot and sexy because women and men gave him their room numbers at least three times a day. They were relentless, especially when we were relaxing in the hot tub. They all wanted us to party with them and have a drink with them. Of course, we never did because during the entire cruise I stayed pissed off at Tony most of the time. By the last day of our cruise, Tony felt like he was the only rooster in the henhouse and asked me if we could book another cruise next year. I told him, "Hell no! Get your clothes on so that we can get off this cruise from hell and get the hell out of here." I was over it and could not wait to get home and back to New Orleans.

Tony and I had so many good stories and some sad stories. Tony had so many times to redeem himself but did not. So many times he had help from me and other people who really loved him. Instead of accepting help and wanting to help himself get off the pain pills, he took the pills anyway. He not only lost respect from me but from his entire family as well.

All Tony had going for him was his good looks, charming personality, book sense, Spanish accent, beautiful dark eyes and perfect olive skin, and of course let's not forget why I named him "Tony the Ten-Inch Pony." I'm ashamed to say, but that's the one reason my four-year marriage lasted that long! Shame on me for being that shallow woman when I was married to him! The things we ladies do to stay married to a good-looking man—only to find out that without respect, the looks fade with only the outside shell of a man remaining. Forgetting that it's what is inside a man's heart, his morals, his pride, and most of all his willingness to be a good person so that he can be good to you! Don't forget what my dad said, "Always look at their shoes. It will be a sign of the way they will take care of you. If the shoes are new, polished, not dull and worn down on the heel and soles, that is a good sign to always look for first when you check him out."

Thank God I was able to move on with my life and open my eyes to seeing beyond the surface of a good-looking man and maybe next time if I did get another chance, I would see the real man that I hope I will have one day. But first, I planned to take a few years off from men to find out who I was as a woman. I prayed that I could get beyond the shallow surface of wanting young eye candy instead of wanting a real man. I sure hoped I'd like what I saw and learn how to love and trust again. I hoped I wouldn't make the same mistakes again. I knew I had certainly learned a hard lesson from my marriage to Tony. From now on, I was going to trust that little voice inside of me that was always telling me the right thing to do. That same little voice that kept telling me, *Bad shoes, bad boy, bad idea, just run away!* I again had to make things right with God and put Him first. My soul got lost in a sin city of parties, drinking, and having as much fun as I could have living in my favorite city in the world, New Orleans. I wanted to still have fun but also get my life back on track. I again hoped and prayed for His forgiveness for letting sex and eye candy cloud my vision and my good judgment.

Saying good-bye to Adam and Lee was so hard. I would miss my best friends who made me laugh each and every day and brought me back to life again. Adam lined up one last marching parade for me to be in before I departed from the Big Easy. The surprise for all the conventioneers for this Mardi Gras parade was for Coco and me to be out front leading them. Of course, I had on my mask so that I could act a fool, and Coco had on her Mardi Gras outfit too. At only two pounds, she stole the show, and more pictures were taken of her than the famous Excelsior Brass Band. We had so much fun as we marched down the middle of Bourbon Street and onto the riverboat for dinner. Adam, Lee, Coco, and I made a night of it one last time before I moved to Atlanta and a not-so-colorful lifestyle.

If only we would have called HBO to let them know, we could have had the best reality show that television had ever seen. I was the Southern princess, Adam and Lee were the two queens, and Classic Concepts Salon/ Spa was the best movie set ever. I never knew when those two old queens were going to break out in song, dance, or drag at any moment. God, I will miss those old fools, and they sure are going to miss me just as much. I made them both feel normal, or as normal as I was. I can hear Mama saying now, "God love my blue baby who thinks she is normal. Bless her heart." I loved Adam and Lee for being different, colorful, and so much damn fun. Going to work at the shop every day was like an adventure. I never knew who I would be working on at any given moment. I worked on hotel guests—including some of the Saints football players because they would stay at the hotel during games and especially during the Super Bowl. I worked on actors who stayed at the hotel like Gene Hackman, G.W. Bailey, Rebecca Wells, Kevin Sorbo, the Backstreet Boys, Geraldo Rivera, and the list goes on and on.

I even got so close to meeting Bill Clinton that I could tell how good he smelled, when he was staying at the Fairmont Hotel. Before I met him (almost), I ran home from work to put on my best business suit so that I could look official. I also put on my nametag that said, "Linnie Delmar— Licensed Massage Therapist—Hotel InterContinental." I looked really professional, or so I thought. I stole an American Express big envelope from the hotel. In the official-looking envelope I had a letter telling him all about me and my unique massage treatment. I also told him about all the movie stars I had worked on. I even went to the trouble of making copies of the pictures of some of the movie stars to prove to him how famous Linnie Delmar was, and that he had to meet me before he left town.

All the streets were blocked and no one was allowed near the Fairmont Hotel. As I got there, he was getting into his car. I yelled out to him, in my horrible-sounding Alabama hick voice, "Mr. President, I need to give you this envelope." I was within a few feet from him. He looked up and smiled at me before he got into his car and rode away. No one arrested me. Only a few people looked at me funny when I wanted to hand deliver an envelope to the president of the United States. It was just like when I was walking through the Pentagon with my black halter top and white shorts on and my official badge clipped to me. No one stopped me! I walked right by the New Orleans police just like they weren't there. I guess I looked official, and this time I didn't have my VIP tag clipped to my black halter top. Instead, I had a nametag clipped to my black Calvin Klein business suit—a nametag that I had made for myself across the street from the hotel at a local printing shop.

I walked right by the Secret Service agents like they weren't even there. When the president's car drove away, I went into action by asking the doorman where he was going. He said that they were going to have dinner at Emeril's. I was running down the street in my business suit and high heels looking like a crazy woman. I had to get to Emeril's restaurant before he did. I knew all the shortcuts, but finally I got a cab. I walked right past the New Orleans police who were blocking the streets. I made it there before his car arrived in less than ten minutes. None other than Emeril himself was standing at the door to greet the president. Again, I guess I looked official, and he opened the door and asked me if he could help me. I said, "Yes. I am Linnie Delmar, and President Clinton left this very important Federal Express envelope at the hotel. Can you please give it to him when he arrives?" He looked into my blue eyes and said, "Miss Delmar, I will personally hand it to him as soon as he gets here." He never looked at my nametag. My mission was accomplished, so I ran back to my hotel as fast as I could. I stayed there all afternoon waiting for the phone to ring. In Linnie's World of hopes and dreams, I just knew I would be working on President Clinton and giving him a relaxing treatment after dinner, and maybe Hillary too! No telling what Bill thought when Emeril handed him an envelope about massage therapy—and more importantly, what did Hillary think of Emeril giving it to him?

I am glad I did not get arrested by the Secret Service or killed by Emeril for handing him important information about Linnie Delmar being the best LMT in the Big Easy! I never got to work on President Clinton or Hillary, but I made sure before they left New Orleans they knew who Linnie Delmar was! When they wanted a massage treatment, I was ready and willing. I still hope one day our paths will cross again, and I can get to meet them and give them the best massage they have ever had. With the stress they both are under on a daily basis, they need me more than any two people have ever needed me before. This was again another Forrest Gump moment of being in the right place at the right time that I will cherish forever.

I will miss being in New Orleans during Mardi Gras, but especially New Year's Eve, where every year was just as special as the last. One of the best was when we all went to our favorite dance club on Bourbon Street called Oz. One year, I was standing within a few feet of Blondie as she sang her ass off, and she wore a dress that looked like it was made with over three thousand razor blades. Of course the razor blades were plastic, but they sure looked real. After leaving there, we walked back down Bourbon Street only to hear Harry Connick Jr. playing the piano in a jazz club. It was moments like those that made New Orleans my favorite city of all. I stayed on a natural high even after my divorce. In the Big Easy, it was hard not to fall in love with the sound of the music, smells of the food, love of the colorful people who loved to party and live life to the fullest. It did make me sad to have to leave, but I knew after the dust settled I would be back as often as I could to visit all my friends and my favorite places that felt like home. My divorce from Tony was final on December 8, 1999. By January of 2000, I had moved away from New Orleans to start over again in Atlanta. This was the beginning for me and my little dog Coco of feeling safe and being close to the real love of my life—my son, Rodney.

He has always been there for me no matter what mistakes I made. The close relationship we had only becomes closer as we both grow older and much wiser. I have learned from my many mistakes, and most of all, I have finally found out who the real Linnie Delmar is. I am and always will be a good person who loves God and puts Him first in her life. He has always been able to shine that light on my path to a good life of helping people and loving them each and every day by using my gift of pampering stressed-out people. I continue to love and cherish the time I spend with my devoted family and wonderful friends who support me and love me dearly as much as I love them.

Chapter 9

MOVING TO ATLANTA AND STARTING OVER AGAIN

Rodney flew down to New Orleans from Atlanta for the last time before my move to Atlanta to say good-bye to Adam and Lee. He also went with me to say good-bye to my wonderful in-laws who were like my real family because they loved me and Rodney so much. It was hard to tell them that I could not take one more day of being married to their son. After four long years of trying hard, I had to let him go because of his drug problem. Tony's mom, who looked just like Joan Collins, looked me in the eye and told me that she didn't know how I was able to take it that long. She didn't blame me one minute for leaving him. She looked at Tony's dad and told him in a firm voice, "He is not moving in here with us. Don't even think about it." His dad and his mom cried as we all hugged and said good-bye. They knew we would never see each other again. I thanked them for all they had done for me and for Tony and for taking us on a trip of a lifetime to Mexico for two weeks. I thanked them for taking good care of me when I almost died of food poisoning not once but twice. Tony's mom stayed by my side the whole time I was in the hospital and wouldn't leave me there alone. They thanked me for taking Tony on vacations he would always remember. His mom told us that Tony told them all about our trip to Disney World. I'm certain Tony never told them about the nude cruise we took after we left Disney World. I thought to myself, for God's sake, I was such a good mommy, I had to take my husband to Disney World! (Although I wanted to go as much or more than he did.) We all hugged and ended our conversation about some of the good memories of our marriage. I left them on pleasant terms, and I said my last good-bye to the extended family I loved dearly and always will.

In later years, I found out that Tony did have to move in with his parents. Years later, he was able to get his own place, a good job, and he was off the pain pills ... or so I heard. I do wish him well. Even though we were married for four years and during the four years we did have moments when we were happy, I have no desire to ever see him again. Rodney drove my car back to Atlanta after the moving van left with all of my furniture in it.

Tony surprised me at the airport before my flight. He told me he had to wish me farewell and good luck before I left New Orleans. He gave me some beautiful tulips because he knew they were my favorite and walked me to the gate. As I told him good-bye and good luck, we both knew we would never see each other ever again. It was finally over, and after all he put me through I still had to tell him I tried to make it work but I couldn't take it any longer. He took full responsibility that it was his fault that it didn't work. He said he was so sorry that he was such a terrible husband! The last words he said to me I remember well: "Thank you for trying to help me. You were the best wife, friend, and lover I will ever have. It is a loss that will haunt me more than my drug problem ever will. I love you, and I always will. I also loved it when you called me Tony the Pony, it always made me laugh and made me feel like Mr. Big." After we hugged, I left Tony standing there in tears and flew from New Orleans to Atlanta. I knew then I would never hear those words "I love you" again from my husband or from any man, for a long time or maybe ever. I would miss that.

Now in the present day, those three little words do not mean as much to me as they used to. Anyone can say "I love you," but the three words I hunger to hear more than ever are still, "You're the one." If I ever hear those little words—or yet even better, four little words, "Linnie, you're the one"—I will feel like my journey has been complete and my life fulfilled with those four words coming from a man who has found me and wants to keep me happy for the rest of my life. My desire to ever get married again is gone, and I doubt the desire will ever return. Actually, I'm okay with that, because my life and the way I want to live it is a lot better when I'm single. If I hear the words "Linnie, you're the one" and I'm a single woman, that would make me happier than if I were married.

When I moved to Atlanta, I was fifty-two. I had no clue how to find my way around the largest city I had ever lived in. I was used to walking everywhere in New Orleans. I moved into a two-bedroom apartment located behind the Ritz-Carlton in Buckhead. My focus was to just make it one day at a time. Coco and I had time on our hands to settle in and get to know our new home in our new city with our new outlook on our new life. I took full advantage of the time I had before I started my new job, so I invited Rodney to go to Key West with me, and he said yes.

We flew to Key West for a long weekend. I have been a scuba diver for many years, and I had the opportunity to dive the site of the famous 1622 treasure ship named the *Atocha*. Mel Fisher discovered where it sunk on July 20, 1985. The estimated value was over $450 million, known as the "*Atocha* Mother Lode." It included forty tons of gold and silver, 100,000 Spanish silver coins, Columbian emeralds, gold and silver artifacts, and 1,000 silver bars. As large as it was, this was only half of the treasure that went down with the *Atocha*. Still missing are 300 silver bars and eight bronze cannons, among other silver and gold. I happened to again be in the right place at the right time when I met Kane Fisher in his office at the Mel Fisher Museum in Key West. I became an investor. I received from the investment thirteen silver coins along with the certificate of authenticity on all thirteen, plus the silver coin I found on my dive. It was a scuba-diving experience of a lifetime and another exciting adventure in the life of Linnie Delmar. Rodney did his own thing while I was on my dive. We both had the time of our lives, together again.

When we got back to our real life in Atlanta, I was able to start my new job with a relaxing attitude adjustment and a good tan. I was hired as an LMT working at the Cherokee Town and Country Club in Buckhead. It was in the wealthiest part of the city of Buckhead on West Paces Ferry, located right down the road from the governor's mansion in Atlanta. I convinced the human-resources department at the club that my technique was so different and so special that I had to have my own treatment room. I did not want to share a room with the other three LMTs who had been working there for years. My boss told me my room would be ready the following day.

I wasn't going to share a room because Linnie Delmar was the famous Massage Therapist to the Stars. Of course, all the other LMTs hated me, and they continued to share this tiny little room that had no personality to it whatsoever. On moving day, I had movers deliver all my massage equipment and custom massage table and set up my personal treatment room. It was as big as my master bedroom. I also brought all my art to hang on the walls so that I would feel right at home and so would my clients. Of course, the other LMTs were pissed off and really hated me even more when they saw how charming, warm, and cozy my room was. I knew they were not going to be my new best friends anytime soon.

Rodney wanted me to learn how to get around the city by taking the MARTA train, which I felt really comfortable with since I had used the train system before when Rich and I were in London and Paris. I loved taking the MARTA everywhere and saw so many interesting people every time I rode it. Rodney worked in midtown Atlanta selling real estate. He and his partner were redoing a large home in College Park. Every weekend, I stayed busy helping them with the renovation on their house, and I loved all the changes he was making on this beautiful historic home.

Rodney has always been so much more mature than me in every way. He has been like the parent and me more like the child most of the time, and to this day he does not give me any slack. He is always the first one to point out my weak points and the things I could improve on. He said that if and when I did meet another man, he had to approve the guy first before we could go out. I do trust his judgment and level head on knowing how to deal with people. He is a wise man at such a young age, and he has his hands full with his mama now living in the same city. I cherished the time with him then and now; as I have gotten older, I make each day count when I'm with him.

I made new friends pretty fast as I always have in the past after any of my divorces. Starting over in Atlanta was a challenge for me. My new best friend's name was Angela, and she worked at a spa at the nearby mall. She lived in a condo in Buckhead not far from where my apartment was. Every Friday after work, she and I would walk to the movies in Phipps Plaza. It was the nicest place to see a movie in our high-price neighborhood. We would usually eat somewhere before the show, at a different place each time. She introduced me to some really nice local restaurants in Buckhead. She was from Macon but had lived in Atlanta for over ten years, so she knew her way around. I was literally lost most of the time trying to find my way around the city when I wasn't with Angela or Rodney. I missed New Orleans and being able to walk everywhere. I couldn't do that in Atlanta, and for weeks Rodney had to drive me everywhere I went except to work.

I settled into my job at the country club, and every day was far different from working with Adam and Lee at the hotel. I had a high-end clientele, mostly rich stay-at-home moms who played tennis at the club. I had to be on my toes, and I knew I couldn't screw up or kid around like I used to with my fellow employees in New Orleans. I had to get serious and get the word out about my pampering package to all the rich uptight ladies who needed it the most. That meant that I had to learn as much as I could about the hot-stone therapy they all requested. I had been using hot stones for years. I had to have an edge over all the other LMTs I worked with. The word got around quickly that the way Miss Linnie used her hot stones all over the body was very different from any therapist they had ever been to. It was different all right—because with every Buckhead Betty (that's the name I gave to all my rich ladies) I worked on, I had no clue what in the hell I was doing from one hot stone to the next. But they loved it! I did whatever the hell I was in the mood for with each client, and it worked.

One time, though, I let the stones get too hot, and when I dropped one out of my hand, it landed next to a candle. The candle fell next to a dry towel, and the towel caught fire! It was like a snowball effect. I had a Buckhead Betty on my custom massage table, and she had no idea that we had a fire in the room. I had managed to get her good and relaxed and, unless she couldn't smell the smoke, I have no idea how she never said a word or moved until it was over. I was a nervous wreck knowing that I almost burned down the oldest, most prestigious country club in Atlanta with Miss Buckhead Betty still on the table. Having so much experience with the hot stones, I didn't panic. I threw some water on the fire until it went out. I even got water all over Miss Buckhead Betty's hair, and she still didn't move or say a word. For a moment I thought she was dead from all the smoke in the room, but when she finally got up, I knew she was okay. Believe it or not, she never said a word. To my surprise, she left me a huge tip! Thank God I missed losing my job that day, and I felt bad that I could have lost a Buckhead Betty along the way, too. That only happened once, thank God, and from that day forward, I made sure I did not screw up like that again. The management liked me, and so did the country-club members. I wanted to keep it that way. It was like another world working there instead of working at the shop in New Orleans with my two old fools and best friends, Adam and Lee. I stayed at the club for another year until they had to do some major renovation in the spa area. I hoped it was not because of all the smoke damage I caused! Because of the renovations, I had to move to another spa, and so did the other LMTs.

I found another job at a spa located off Piedmont in Buckhead. It was a very small elite day spa named Chinsea. For the life of me, I could never pronounce the name of it correctly. The owner was a lady who was very nice and was willing to give me a larger commission than I made at the country club. I loved that, because my rent was so high living in Buckhead. In the year 2000, I paid twelve hundred dollars per month for a two-bedroom apartment that backed up to a toll road. I had a lot of traffic noise—but compared to the noise living in the French Quarter, the noise in Atlanta was mild, and I didn't pay any attention to it. One busy day at Chinsea, I happened to be put in charge of answering the phone while the owner left and I was in between clients. It was a job that I dreaded, because I had no clue how to say the word "Chinsea." My first call just happened to be from Rodney, who was calling to ask me out to lunch. Instead of saying, "Chinsea Body Spa," I answered the phone and said, "Chintzy Day Spa, this is Linnie, can I help you?"

Rodney, in shock and horror, yelled out on the phone, "Mama, my God, you just said 'Chintzy Day Spa' instead of 'Chinsea Body Spa.'" He went on, "For God's sake, and to keep them from firing your country ass, you have got to learn how to say it right before you get another phone call. Thank goodness it was me calling instead of a client or, worse, your boss." He said in his firm outside voice, "Mama, this is a big city, and if you screw up like that they will fire your country ass in a heartbeat and won't think twice about it."

After that moment and lots of practice, I learned how to say it correctly: "Chinsea Body Spa, this is Linnie, can I help you?"

Working at "Chintzy Day Spa," I was making pretty good money because I worked on six or seven clients a day on average. After only six months, the bottom fell out. Chinsea had to close its doors because the owner's boyfriend, who was also her CPA, had been taking money from her the whole time she owned the spa. He was buying drugs—pain pills. She had to close because she could no longer pay her bills or pay us. We had only thirty days to pack up and leave and find another job. My poor boss lady's world was a disaster, and my heart felt so bad for her. I knew how it felt to lose a loved one to drugs because of Tony the Pony's addiction to pain pills. She was a strong business lady, and she assured us that she would be fine after the dust settled. It was time for me to hit the ground running again to find another good job. I felt bad that I had to say good-bye to "Chintzy Day Spa"—just kidding, Rodney!

I ended up in midtown Atlanta at a boutique-style salon and day spa named Salon R. Julian. It was decorated so beautifully, and it was the perfect place for me to be. They welcomed me with open arms. The owner's name was Ron Carter, and of course he was gay. We became the best of friends from day one. To this day, we are still the best of friends, and he still is my hairstylist, too. Ron was known to be the best hairstylist in Atlanta. A haircut with him was expensive, but it would be the best haircut you could get in the city. His clients were loyal, rich, and loved him. I loved him too, because he gave me a job just in time for me to pay the high rent on my apartment. I still couldn't believe I had to pay that much for rent every month. Rodney kept telling me, "Welcome to the big city of Atlanta," and expensive rent was normal. I had to get used to it, though, because this was my life now. All I seemed to be doing was working at least ten to twelve hours a day. I was tired all the time just to pay my rent. Being tired was good in a way, though, because it kept my mind off of not having a man in my life and not having sex anymore. I was comfortable with that and accepted that because, after all, I was in the process of finding the real Linnie. I was slowly finding out that I was a pretty cool lady and a very hard worker. At my new location in midtown, I took on a few new clients who were far different from the Buckhead Bettys I had worked on at the country club.

I was getting some cross-dressers and transvestites (called trannies in the gay world) and of course lots of gay people. I loved each and every one of them, and they loved Miss Linnie, too. I loved the fact that each and every day I never knew who was going to be on my table next, It made me feel right at home, just like being in New Orleans again on a typical day at the Classic Concepts Salon/Spa with Adam and Lee. God, I missed those old fools, and meeting my new colorful friends filled a void for me. I felt right at home again. I was not only able to do the pampering package on them once a week, but I also gave my more colorful male clients tips on how to do their makeup and hair. I also told them when buying clothes, please stay away from Spandex as much as possible, due to their big manly body parts might not look as good as they think they do. They loved the fact that I had just moved from New Orleans and that I was up on all the latest fashions for drag. They loved me even more when I told them that one of my best friends was "Miss Viagra" or "Miss Vi" (Lee)—the most famous drag queen in all of New Orleans! Of course, I told them time and time again, less is more and stay in rooms with not a lot of bright lights that might show off some of their imperfections. They agreed, and they loved candlelight just as much as I did, if not more!

My new friends told me about the church they attended, and I ended up joining a wonderful, mostly gay United Methodist Church in midtown. They welcomed everyone with open arms, and they had no rules on who wanted to hear the word of God as far as race, creed, or the color of someone's skin, and most of all it didn't matter if you were gay or straight. I fell in love with my new church family, and they loved Miss Linnie, too.

It was called St. Mark's United Methodist Church. It was the closest to being like my favorite church in the whole world, which is Glide Memorial Methodist Church in San Francisco where the famous Rev. Cecil Williams is the pastor. I can feel the love as soon as I walk in the door of that church. They accept everyone no matter who they were, rich or poor, gay or straight, famous movie stars or homeless people. It does not matter, and I loved that feeling I get of love and happiness. I felt the same happiness and joy at my new church in Atlanta. I loved it so much that I even joined the choir. I went to the service on Sunday and dinners every Wednesday night. Choir practice was an experience, to say the least. Just like Glide Memorial Methodist Church, the talent that was in that choir was overwhelming, and I loved being just a small part of that joy every week. My life even felt more complete by joining this wonderful church. My dream one day is to get to sing in the choir at Glide in San Francisco. The pastor, Cecil Williams, and his wife are very dear people to me, and I visit with both of them when I go to San Francisco to stay with my best friend Bettie, who is also a member there. Bettie introduced them to me and also to Glide Memorial Methodist Church many years ago. Rich and I, when we were married, loved staying at Bettie's beautiful apartment located in Russian Hill in the heart of San Francisco. Bettie was the best tour guide we could have ever wished for because she had lived there since 1968 and knew the city like the back of her hand. Bettie has been my best friend since we were in the ninth grade in high school. To this day, she is still one of the most unique and special women in my life, along with Barbara, Theresa, Rhoda, and Sue and Tammy Hopper. They are all like sisters to me!

I had now been living in Atlanta for over two years and in my second year in the choir at St. Marks's. Before Easter Sunday, we were practicing some new songs that were in Latin. I kept telling the choir that since all of them read music and I was the only one who did not, I might just sit this one out. Of course, they told me it was okay and to just move my mouth and lip synch. I was thinking to myself, if they only knew how many times I had done that already. Everyone in the choir was so talented and so nice to me. I felt like the oddball with such special talented people around me every Sunday, even if they did put me front and center in our seating arrangements. Rodney would attend church with me sometimes. He would tell me after church, "Mama, you can tell that you aren't doing it right, and you are just moving your mouth with nothing coming out. Aren't you afraid they will find out that you do not know anything about music or singing?" I told him they already knew but told me they don't care because I looked so good sitting in the middle of them. I was always smiling and just happy to be there every Sunday. Even if I screwed up every now and then, they said that it was okay because I was so honest and so much damn fun to be with.

My lease was up on my expensive apartment in Buckhead. I was ready and willing to look for a less-expensive place that was closer to where I worked in midtown. Rodney and I began our search, and as usual, he made it such a fun adventure for both of us every time we went to look at a new apartment. Rodney was one of the top salesmen for the best and largest realty company in Atlanta. I was sure he would find the perfect apartment for me and Coco. In our search, we came across one nice two-bedroom apartment that was within walking distance of everything that midtown had to offer. There was only one catch: there were no dogs allowed. Most apartments did allow dogs less than twenty pounds. When we met with the owner of this very small charming complex, Rodney told me that I had to tell her about Coco. At first I did not even want to bring it up, since Coco weighed less than five pounds. But since Rodney was so honest and went strictly by the book and by the rules, I knew I had to fess up to her that yes I do have a dog. I wanted this place so bad! I told her I do have a very small dog! Before I could even get it out of my mouth that Coco is old and she never barks (which was a total lie), she again told me no dogs allowed in a firm harsh outside voice. Rodney was so embarrassed when I could not let it go. The next words out of my mouth were that Coco used a pee pad because her pee and poops are so tiny. Rodney, with shock and horror on his face, gave me that "go to hell" look that meant, *Mama, please shut up and don't say another word!* He told the lady he was so sorry, and we were leaving. When we got back to the car, he told me that it did not sweeten the pot by telling this nice lady that Coco would pee and shit on her beautiful hardwood floors using a pee pad. He told me, "Remember, Mama, you are in the big city, and she could give a shit about Coco due to she had already told you no dogs." I never was good with rules and still have a hard time following them by the book like Rodney and my sister Valerie do. In Linnie's World, a small tiny little thing like Coco was an exception to any stupid apartment rules. I ended up finding a nice place that did accept dogs, and I moved in right away and loved it.

One day, while having lunch at one of my favorite places in College

Park that's close to the Atlanta airport named the Barbecue Kitchen, I saw a beautiful Harley-Davidson Road King sitting outside the front door. I asked the owner, Don, about the bike, and he said it belonged to a friend of his named Dick. So Don introduced me to Dick that day. Dick was a riding partner with Don, who was also a Harley man—he and his wife, Barbara, loved to ride. When I met Dick, we talked about motorcycles—and before I knew it, he asked me to go riding with him sometime. His wife had just died a few months earlier, and he was trying to get used to being single and alone again. I assured him that as time went on, it gets better and better. Although I was not looking for a Dick to ride with, I wanted to ride his Harley-Davidson. For years, I had always been a Harley wannabe. Now was my chance to have a new friend and fulfill my dream of riding like the wind and have that feeling of being free. I even had some Harley clothes already. We rode most every weekend up in the north Georgia mountains around Helen, Georgia, and I loved my new passion for riding and hoped one day I would own my own Harley-Davidson.

Rodney was so worried when I went riding, not just because it was dangerous, but because he did not know my new friend Dick very well. Rodney did not like the fact that I was taking off with a strange man I knew nothing about. All I knew was that he liked to ride motorcycles as much as I did, and in my mind that made it all right. Plus, he was rich and single. I tried my best to look at Dick as more than a riding partner, but there was no chemistry whatsoever, so we remained just friends. When I had turned fifty, I'd had to have a hysterectomy. I had no interest in sex anymore. It was the first time in my life that sex did not rule my mind and body. I was okay with the fact that now that I was in my early fifties, that part of my life was over. Having sex anymore was gone, and I didn't even miss it. It had been almost three years or more that I had gone without sex, and I really didn't miss it or think about it anymore. For me to make a statement like that after my entire life of having sex most every day with my husbands and lovers, I should get some kind of award or something.

On the other hand, Dick, I'm sure, would have loved us being more than just riding partners and just friends. He was older than me, and thank God, sex was never an issue that was even brought up in our relationship. It didn't matter anyway, because we were having fun with the wind in our hair, sun on our faces, and the love to ride and freedom to do it as often as possible when I wasn't working at the spa.

I will never forget the morning of September 11, 2001. I was getting ready for work and had my favorite morning show, *The Today Show*, on TV when the world changed forever! I called Rodney to hurry up and turn on his television, and he had already heard the news. Like me, he could not believe this was really happening before our eyes on national live television. We both stayed on the phone with each other and saw the second plane hit the tower, and we both screamed out in horror. We both knew that our wonderful country was in trouble and wondered what would happen next. The last thing I wanted to do was go to work and pamper people all day when this was the worst day in the history of our country.

I made myself go anyway so that I wouldn't be fired, and before my workday was over, they sent everyone home to be with their loved ones. Rodney and I were together for the next few days. All I wanted to do was get in my car and go to New York City to help my fellow Americans in their time of need. If nothing else, I was going to do mini-massages with my high-touch massage chair in tow to work on all the volunteers looking for their loved ones. I was willing to do anything to help out in any way I could and in any place that needed me. To this day, I wish I had gone up there, but then I had no money and my boss probably would have fired me because I had clients depending on me. After 9/11, I felt guilty about taking a ride with Dick on the Harley and having such a good time being relaxed. So many families were hurting and in so much pain over the loss of their loved ones. I never saw my riding buddy and friend Dick again. I did not know at the time that it would be years before I would ever be on another motorcycle, and it would not be a Harley-Davidson, it would be a Honda touring bike, a Gold Wing, which is top of the line of all motorcycles.

Out of the clear blue sky, I got a phone call from my mama. She asked me if I was over living in the big city yet. I asked her why, and she told me that after twelve years, the renters had finally moved out of one of her rental houses in Fairhope. She asked me if I wanted to move back home. She told me that the house would be big enough for my home and for my business. I was so happy that she asked and happier to know that I could finally move back home so I could help take care of my parents if they needed me. I had never lived as far away as Atlanta before, and I missed Mama and Dad more than I thought I would. I was more than ready to move back home to be near them.

My lease was up on my apartment around the same time she called, so on July 15, 2002, I was on my way back home to sweet home Alabama. I would miss Rodney a lot, but I knew this move was meant to be. I was also ready to be my own boss and open my own day spa. I was hoping I would also get all my old clients back from when I was working with the Grand Hotel Marriott for over nine years. I had been gone for over eight years, and I was ready to start over again and come full circle. I was coming home to the Redneck Riviera, where this wonderful ride of a life all began.

With all the experience of working with the Grand Hotel Marriott for over nine years and the InterContinental in New Orleans for over six years, and working with more than ten motion-picture production companies and A-list actors, I felt like anything was possible. I was physically at the top of my game at the age of fifty-four. From working at Cherokee Town and Country Club and the Spa in Atlanta, working on seven clients every day five days a week, I was strong and healthy as a bull and felt great.

Some changes had been made to the Grand Hotel Marriott. They had built a million-dollar spa. I was worried that all my contacts at the hotel had moved on. They might not be there any longer to send me hotel guests. If they were still there after eight years of me being gone, they wouldn't be able to send me people because they had to be loyal to the new Grand Hotel Marriott spa.

I had my faith in God to help me start my new life again, and with my faith and positive attitude I was just going to let it be in His hands now and pray for the best. I was glad that He had blessed me with my excellent health and the gift He had given to me to still love my job of pampering stressed-out people who enjoyed my unique style and techniques. I had an additional eight years of advanced skills to add to my trade of being a professional Licensed Massage Therapist. While working in Atlanta, I also had an opportunity to teach my technique to a couple of the instructors who worked at the Atlanta School of Massage. They wanted to learn my technique so that they could pass it on to the students who wanted to own their own business as an LMT. In Linnie's World, I knew I was not only Fairhope's first Licensed Massage Therapist, but I still held the title of the best massage therapist and let's not forget, Massage Therapist to the Stars!

Chapter 10

MOVING BACK HOME
TO FAIRHOPE AND
STARTING OVER AGAIN

I was now fifty-four years old, and here I was starting another new chapter of my life with a new home and a brand-new business. I moved into a charming renovated 1910 home that had four bedrooms and two bathrooms. I was so overwhelmed that I almost had a breakdown from pure joy in front of Mama, Dad, and my sisters Kim and Valerie. They were all there to welcome Coco and me back home with open arms and happy hearts. I was finally back home and was safe again in the arms of my family. I still couldn't believe that Mama was going to let me move into one of her prime rental houses in a prime location. I planned to pay her a quarter of the rent she was used to getting. I had a lot of painting and fixing up to do to have it feel like mine. Rodney came down from Atlanta to help with what he called "the fun part." I had every picture hung and every box put up in less than three days and made it look like I had been living there for at least ten years—for all of which I have my OCD and organizing skills to thank.

Now I had my work cut out to start working on getting some of my old clients back and some new clients, too, so that my day spa would be a success. I was willing to give out a lot of complimentary pampering packages in order to get some regular clients coming in at least once a month. I again turned to my wonderful friend Kenny McLean, who was the one person who was there to help me from the very beginning in 1986. He was there for me again when I needed him the most to let all of his friends know I was back. He was so glad that his favorite massage therapist was finally home to stay this time. Kenny's friends were willing to help me spread the word about my new day spa. In a town like Fairhope, as quaint and charming as it is, it is all about who you know—and they knew everyone. I started calling some of my old clients from over eight years ago. They all had the same phone numbers and started coming to me again.

Even with the support of friends and family and a wonderful article coming out in the *Mobile Press-Register* on September 18, 2002, that told about my years away and my new business, it was a struggle each and every month. Mama had even given me a year to get settled without charging me any rent. I still could not seem to get my head above water with all my new expenses of starting my day-spa business. I had to get some serious money coming in and soon.

I decided that for one year, I would go to work at the Grand Casino in Biloxi, Mississippi. They had a million-dollar spa and they hired me on the spot. I was willing to work on seven people a day for five days on and two days off in order to get on my feet enough to start my business in Fairhope the way I wanted to. At fifty-four years old, I was the oldest massage therapist they had ever hired. Because of my twenty-plus years experience and worked with more than ten motion-picture companies, they were anxious for me to start work as soon as I could. I was also older than most of the management in my entire department. They liked me, and I was willing to give them 100 percent and the best year I could give them.

Every day for the next year, I would leave Fairhope by nine in the morning and drive to Biloxi. After a long eight-hour shift, I would get home by nine in the evening. By the end of my long shift and my seventh client, I was just about ready to slap some people around. I was ready to get the hell out of there. I had built up my muscles to the point that when I worked on some of my clients, they would yell out for me to back off just a tad. I was as strong as an ox.

On the long ride home every night, all I could think about was my comfortable bed waiting on me to crawl into it. The next morning, the routine would start all over again. I looked forward to coming home because it made me feel like I had taken a rental house (one of Mama's best) and made it into a warm charming cozy home/business for me and my little dog, Coco, who stayed with Mama and Dad when I was at work. Every piece of furniture I had fit into each room looked like I had chosen the pieces for that room and for that spot to place them in. Mama even had some custom-made linen drapes stored away, and when we got them out and hung them they all fit perfectly on the existing rods in every room. Another sign I was meant to be where I was at that time in my life.

I had been in such small apartments for so many years now that having all this room to spare was one of my dreams come true. From time to time, it would still overwhelm me how Mama's love and kindness came to my rescue again when I needed her. Even working all those hours at the Grand Casino was not so bad when I always had my beautiful home to come back to and the love of Mama and Dad. They lived about two miles away in a very nice retirement community named Homestead Village.

My trip back and forth to Biloxi became a normal routine for me, and I loved my new job at the Bayview Hotel, where the Bellisimo Day Spa for the Grand Casino was located. I worked with seven massage therapists, some of whom were right out of massage school. They called me Miss Linnie, and I was always giving them good ideas on how to increase their tips by giving their clients more than what they paid for. They called me their mentor, and I loved that I could share some of my massage experience with them. Our salary was average, but we depended on tips to make up for our hourly wage. All of us depended on getting big tips from the high rollers. When some of the hosts working at the casino hotel found out about me being Massage Therapist to the Stars, they began to send me more and more high-rollers. That made me happy, because high rollers tip good. I went from making a lot of money in New Orleans and Atlanta to having to worry about how much I made on tips each day. Even if I was considered a big deal, working on all the movie stars up until this point in my life, here they could give a damn because it was dog-eat-dog on a daily basis. Everyone had to fend for herself.

At times I would get hundred-dollar tips more than once on an average day. Every night when my eleven-to-seven shift ended, all of the LMTs would sit around a big table in the break room as our boss gave out our tips for the day. Some of them got ten dollars, fifteen, or twenty, sometimes a little more depending. I would get twenty dollars, fifty, or a hundred, and most of the time even more. The other therapists would ask me what in the hell was I doing back there to get those kinds of big tips? My reply was "Always give the client more than they paid for." Put hot towels on them, or use some extra reflexology on their hands and feet, or maybe even some mild facial techniques. They looked at me wondering why they hadn't thought of that.

I explained to the seven of them that we all need to have a hot cabbie in all our massage rooms for our hot towels. I asked them if they minded if I stayed in one room on each client because I hated changing rooms every time for every client. I wanted the same room because I had too much stuff to carry, and I was old. They all said that it was okay with them because I was so old. They felt sorry for me.

I wasn't good at following the rules, and working there was no exception. I brought some things that worked for me from my spa in Fairhope. I didn't tell the management about my hot stones that I used to rub clients down with throughout the fifty minutes we were allotted for each person. The clients were supposed to pay extra for the hot-stone therapy; the hell with that, I threw that in too. I figured since I was only going to be there a year, a hot stone or two couldn't hurt and would increase my tips a lot, which it did. I wanted my clients to get more bang for their buck, and they did and still do here at my day spa in Fairhope.

From the host sending me all their high rollers and VIPs, every day was a new day meeting new people, from Tony Bennett to Vicki Lawrence. I also heard that a dear friend who I had not seen since 1989 when I was his massage therapist on his West Coast tour, Mr. Merle Haggard, was coming in to get a massage. He wanted me to work on him while he was the entertainment at the Biloxi Grand Casino. When they told him I was already booked up, he got mad and canceled his appointment. He wanted me and no one else to work on him. Maybe next time, Merle, if you ever come to Fairhope to my day spa, I will take care of you and your wife, Theresa, too. I felt honored that he even remembered me and felt bad when they couldn't change my schedule so that I could have worked on him. The spa manager was nice, but she wanted everyone to stick to the rules, especially Miss Linnie! Of course, that went in one ear and out the other.

Some of my new LMT friends liked me, and we would occasionally go to shows together—we were given free tickets if the huge Biloxi Grand Theatre wasn't full. We saw some great shows for free. We all hated wearing the uniforms that consisted of tan slacks, white golfing shirt with the spa logo on it, and of course our nametags, all provided free by the casino. They wanted us to look professional. Instead, I looked like a big bull dyke! Really, I looked like the biggest and strongest lipstick lesbian you could imagine, who would do some serious damage on you if you crossed me on a bad day. I had cut my blonde hair off and went back to my natural color, which was a dark auburn, just to give my hair a rest and to see if I had any gray coming in yet. Everyone loved it, especially Mama. I hated it. I had no gray, so of course I went blonde again, and I'm letting it get long. To this day, it is still growing, but when I could afford to buy my Harley I wanted it blowing in the wind as I rode off in the sunset. Free as a bird with only my Harley-Davidson between my firm thighs.

Yes, working at the Grand Casino Spa in Biloxi brought Miss Linnie, the famous Massage Therapist to the Stars, down a notch or two to say the least. It was a humbling experience each and every day for one whole year. But it did me good to know that I could still do a hard day's work. I held my own and kept up with the twenty-year-old LMTs, although it about killed me. I stayed worn out, but I never let on how tired I was and kept them guessing on, how does this old woman do it? I was with the Grand Casino Spa from June 1, 2003, until June 30, 2004, and learned a lot from being at this special place for the year that I was there. They learned a lot, too. I taught the LMTs who wanted to learn my famous technique. I talked the management into put hot cabbies in all the treatment rooms.

I never gambled, but I did roll the dice for one of the high rollers one time, and what an exciting time that was. I did not even know his name, and I would not be able to say it anyway because it was an Asian name. I only met him once when I worked on him at the casino spa. He was either Japanese or Korean. When I was walking through the casino as I was getting off work one evening and going to a show, I saw him in the casino. He asked me to roll the dice for him just once, because I looked so lucky. So I did, and he won over $141,000. I kept rolling the dice for almost an hour. He was a high roller; he knew how to double down and cover all his bets on the crap table. He handed me five thousand-dollar chips and said thank you for being his lucky charm. I was so thrilled and yet shocked at the same time. That was again a Forrest Gump moment of being in the right place at the right time. I needed that five thousand dollars so I could finally quit working there and pay for my move from Atlanta to Fairhope. I could finally buy my spa equipment to start my day spa in Fairhope. That was the best hour that I spent at the Grand Casino, and I left on such a good note with this amazing gambling story to take with me.

In my younger days, while working at The Enclave condo property in Atlantic City, I won another lucky high roller over twenty-one thousand dollars by rolling the dice for him at the Golden Nugget Casino. That man gave me seven hundred dollars, and I did not know his name either. That experience felt just as good as this experience did. The bad-ass famous pit boss "Big Daddy" at the Grand Casino even told me that some people were lucky and just had that special touch going on with the dice. I was one of those special people. I didn't realize at the time that if I'd had on my casino uniform and nametag and was still on the clock, I could have been fired. Thank the good Lord I had changed clothes before putting my lucky hands on those dice! I have not set foot in a casino since my last day of work there.

Biloxi had turned into the little Las Vegas of the South and was growing bigger each year until Hurricane Katrina hit on August 29, 2005. Thank God I quit working there in 2004, because I would have been out of work just like all of my friends were. It was the storm that changed America and changed the Gulf Coast forever. I was so lucky again because my home and spa in Fairhope were spared. It was a catastrophic storm that our area will not soon forget, and my heart aches for all the people who lost everything. I again thank God for my good luck and blessings that I have been given throughout my life. On August 29, 2005, the way I saw my life and the life of others who were not as lucky as me changed due to Hurricane Katrina. I had a chance to help several people I knew from New Orleans find a job and a place to live. I took what good fortune I had and helped them out as much as I was able to. I even found a couple of them new jobs in our Fairhope area.

A few weeks after Hurricane Katrina, I got a phone call. Lo and behold, it was Tony the Pony calling me from New Orleans. I had not seen him or talked to him since our divorce in 1999. He wanted to know if I was okay and if I received any damage to my home in Fairhope. He also asked about my parents, and when I told him we were fine, he let me know his folks were fine too, no damage to their beautiful home in Metairie. After some more small talk about the storm, I asked him if he got off the pain pills. With a lot of excitement in his voice, he told me that he had been clean and sober—off the pills—for over three months now. My heart sank when he told me that. All I could think about was, if I had stayed with him, all these years later I would still have a prescription-drug addict for a husband. He also told me that he had a young daughter from a girl he met in drug rehab. He said that they never married, but he loved being a dad. I told him I was very happy for him. I also told him to say hello to his mom and dad. We said good-bye, and I have never heard from him again nor want to.

Since my business was slow after the hurricane, all I could do was pray for better times and hope that business would pick up, which it finally did. In my spare time, I would watch all the motorcycles go by, wishing I could be riding on one again soon because I missed riding so much. All my tension and stress seemed to leave me because I was so relaxed when I was on a Harley or at this point on any bike. It didn't matter—I just wanted to ride. I was born to ride a motorcycle, and it was all I could think about. I wondered how I could manage to own a bike of my own one day.

Out of the clear blue sky, a dear friend and client named Fran called me. She wanted me to come up to the Fairhope Civic Center and set up to do some mini-massages for the Home Builders Association. They were having their annual Fairhope Home Show. I wasn't busy that Saturday, so I loaded up my high-touch massage chair in my car and off I went to do free mini-massages, hoping to get some new clients who would come in for the hour pampering package. At the end of the day, after doing about seventy-five free five-minute mini-massages, I was tired and ready to slap my last couple of people around just to get the hell out of there. My last person was a big, tall, bald-headed man who got on the chair and, with the spotlight that Fran had placed me under, blinded me with the glare from his bald head. I told him his head was blinding me, and he told me, "Ouch, that hurt!" He began to laugh, and so did I. From that day forward, we have been the best of friends, and we have kept on laughing. His name is Larry, and of all things, he is a biker/businessman and was born to ride just like I was. Thanks to my friend Fran, I met someone who makes me laugh and feel happy to have a special friend like him. After the home show where we first met, I found out that he was from Atlanta and was single because his wife had died a few years earlier. He had been married to her for over thirty years, so I knew he had to have been a good husband. I told him that my son, Rodney, lived in Atlanta in midtown, and he was in real estate, and he was also gay. I asked him if he would have a problem with that. In his nice, soft, wonderful-sounding voice he said that he had always been a people person, and he liked anyone and everyone as long as they were nice to him, it didn't matter if they were gay or straight! He won a few points for that answer, to say the least. He owns his own company in Atlanta with his twin daughters. They sell foam insulation to building contractors all over the country. He has been the best thing that has happened to me in many years. With his help, I have found out how much fun riding can really be. We have traveled from coast to coast on his Honda Gold Wing touring bike pulling a trailer. Most of all, I have found out how much fun life can be when you meet the right man you want to be with and share a life with. Since he is only a year older than me, and he loves life as much as I do, we have a lot in common.

Larry is smart and makes me laugh and lets me be myself, giving me the freedom when I need it for travel or work. He knows about my wild past and my four husbands but has yet to ask one question about either. He respects me as the person I am today, and I respect him for the wonderful father he is to his two daughters and a wonderful grandfather to his two handsome grandsons. He is a strong man and a thirty-second-degree

Mason (just like my dad). He is a man who has always done the right thing for his family, friends, and Masonic brothers. He is like me because he sees the good in people. He is also and great dancer and has taught Miss Linnie some new moves!

After all these many years, I finally know who the real Linnie is, and I am finally complete as the person I have always wanted to be before the men in my life ever found me. Now Larry is a bonus in my life. It took many months of friendship before I would open my heart up for a romantic relationship. I wasn't looking for a man to come along, and that's when he found me. My mama and dad kept telling me to focus on my business and "make as much money as you can while you can. Keep your faith in God and the right man will find you," and that is exactly how he found me, when I least expected him to come along. I love what I do every day, pampering all my clients who are also my friends. Caring for Mama and Dad, who fulfill me with their love and kindness each and every day has also been a bonus. I have finally come full circle back to my roots and am back home where I belong in sweet home Alabama. I can honestly say my life is complete, and I am the happiest I have ever been at the ripe old age of sixty.

My dream came true and on April 7, 2006, I was able to buy an Ultra Classic Harley-Davidson Trike. I named it "Big Boy." I have always had a weakness for the big boys, if you know what I mean. That bike is the love of my life, after Rodney and his "sister," Coco. I feel like such a bad-ass biker every time I take it for a ride. I feel free as the wind, and I feel that my life has been blessed with lots of happiness, sadness, ups and downs. I have had four husbands, and I learned from them all about love, life, and what heartache feels like. They were in my life for a reason, and without that reason, I would not have had all my life experiences to write about in this book. This has been my life "divorced on the Redneck Riviera," and I have cherished every moment, as good and bad as the years have been. I would not have changed one thing if I had it all to do over again. It took this crazy life of mine to find out who Linnie really is.

The odd thing that I still can't figure out is that the "Big Boy" I ride on these days in this time of my life—my Harley-Davidson—has given me almost as much pleasure as some of the big boys I used to ride on years ago.

Believe me when I say they were really big boys—I was married to all four of them. Go figure that one! All I know is that some people are cut out to have one husband, and some of us are cut out to have four husbands. Some of us work hard and live life to the fullest, and every day is an adventure. People like me can still be happy with no husband at all. Like Forrest Gump, I have always said that life is like a box of chocolates—you never know what you are going to get! I have been living proof of that, and I thank God I have lived to tell my story!

Chapter 11

MOVIE STARS THAT MISS LINNIE RUBBED THE RIGHT WAY!

When I began my journey as a Licensed Massage Therapist (LMT) in 1986, I had no idea that, by being in the right place at the right time, I would be writing a book telling some interesting stories of movie stars who I have rubbed the right way. I never imagined my hands would be massaging their bodies on huge movie sets and soundstages while filming a movie. Chapter 5 of this book is when I started meeting and having the opportunity to work on these famous people. I had to find a career that fit me. It wasn't until then that these magic hands became famous, and I became known as Massage Therapist to the Stars in our local newspaper. The headlines read, "Local Massage Therapist Rubs Merle the Right Way!" I was so embarrassed and mortified. I was hoping they would check with me before they labeled it in those words on the front page! It was the part about rubbing Merle the right way that I hated. Showing the photo he gave me didn't matter as much as the headline did. Their only explanation was that it would capture the attention of the people. Well let me tell you right now that in a small town like Fairhope, Alabama, that kind of headline definitely got their attention! Just walking down Fairhope Avenue in the middle of downtown, people would give that very loud good ol' Alabama yell-out, "Hey, Linnie! Are you still rubbing Merle down the right way?" After turning blood red I would just smile, shake my head, and keep on walking. What I really wanted to do was yell back in my outside loud hick voice, "Go to hell, you redneck," but Miss Linnie is good with keeping her cool, so I just kept on walking.

When I met Merle Haggard for the first time, it was at a concert that my girlfriend Gloria and I went to in Myrtle Beach, South Carolina, of all places. We had taken a long weekend trip just to get away. We saw that Merle Haggard was playing at a concert hall, so we bought tickets to see the show. We had no idea that the tickets put us right up front close to the stage.

Before the show started, his manager came out, and I overheard him telling the stage crew that Merle's back had gone out, and he wasn't sure if the show would still go on. When I heard that, I told him that I was an LMT. As fast as I got it out of my mouth, he had me by the hand, taking me back to Merle's bus fondly named Hag One. I asked him if Gloria could come too. He said yes. When we got on the bus, Merle was in pain with his upper and middle back. When I told Merle that I could do some neuromuscular therapy on him, he said that worked for him and get started. I began working on him for thirty minutes, then he looked at his manager and said, "I don't know what this girl did to me, but my pain is gone. Hire her while I'm onstage!"

Gloria looked at me, and I looked at her, and I said, "What in the hell just happened?" She and I started laughing. We were in shock, and I really thought he was kidding.

His manager, Steve, told me, "Merle doesn't joke about things like that, so can you leave with us tonight?" I didn't know what to say because it happened so fast. My gut feeling told me to just leave with them with the clothes on my back and let Gloria drive my car back to Fairhope. My OCD told me, *Oh my God, I can't do that because I have to get things organized with Rodney, get all my massage equipment, clothes, and makeup that I need with me before I can leave to go anywhere.* That was one time where I could have kicked my OCD in the ass, because after Merle got back to the bus for an answer, I had to tell him no. He looked shocked when I told him I couldn't go. He asked why. I told him, and he calmly said that it was too bad, because since this was his East Coast tour, they were on their way to Washington, D.C.

I later found out that they had done a private party at the White House for George and Barbara Bush. I could have been there if only I had gone with my gut feeling instead of my OCD. I felt sicker than ever thinking that I probably would have worked on them too! In Linnie's World, the Lincoln bedroom would have made the perfect place to set up my portable massage table. He told me that since I couldn't go on that tour, they would have their West Coast tour coming up in a couple of months, and he hoped that I could go then. I told him that would work better for me and give me time to prepare. The drive all the way back to Alabama from Myrtle Beach was a long one. I still had that little voice inside of me saying, *Linnie, this was your big chance and you just blew it!*

After a couple of months went by, I got a call from Dana, his daughter. She told me they were flying me out to Sacramento, California, where I would meet them on Merle's bus Hag One to start his West Coast tour. The tour started there and would end up in Pasadena, California, which is northeast of Los Angeles. Then I would fly on to Phoenix, Arizona, and back to Mobile. She also told me her dad was still talking about how I fixed his back. What a compliment—Merle Haggard telling his daughter about me! I was a nervous wreck up until I was on the airplane because it sounded too good to be true, me going on tour with the singing legend Merle Haggard.

Once I arrived in Sacramento and they saw how much massage equipment and luggage I had, they freaked out. They looked at me like, *What in the hell is this crazy woman doing with more luggage than the entire band has put together?* Hag One was loaded to the gills after Miss Linnie came aboard! Merle was a man of few words until he got to know you better, so all he said was, "Girl, all you had to do was show up with those hands of yours. That's the only equipment you're going to need." He was right, because everything on the bus was off the cuff and spur of the moment with him. I either worked on him on his sofa or it could be sitting in the back of the bus at the kitchen table. It didn't matter, because when his back, neck, or shoulders hurt, it was showtime for me to work my magic. I also worked on a few of his band members from time to time like Biff Adams, who was his drummer/bus driver; Dean Holloway; and the one and only Charlie Dick (the late Patsy Cline's husband). I also got to be backstage at every concert, state fair, or rodeo when I wasn't working, which was an experience in itself. Everywhere we stopped along the west coast of California, everyone knew Merle, and if it was a regular stop, he knew all their names too.

Finally we arrived in Phoenix, which was the last stop on the tour. By then, Merle and I were good friends, so he asked me if I wanted to play golf with him and Glen Campbell. Throughout the trip, I told Merle all about Benny the Candy Man teaching me everything there was to know about golf, so I guess that's why he asked me. My gut feeling told me to say yes, but again my OCD kicked in. I missed that small window of opportunity to go play golf because they couldn't wait for me to go change clothes. I wanted an outfit that was suitable for golf instead of my massage uniform that I wore most of the time. That's when I really felt like saying to myself, *Mama, your blue baby just screwed up again!*

About every other night, Hag One would stop at a real nice hotel, and Merle would pay for an entire floor for all of us to have our own room. I would turn my room into a spa. He would get at least a two-hour massage before every concert, and that's when I was on the clock full-time due to other band members wanting at least an hour treatment too. Working for Merle gave me the experience of being able to travel with anyone who was on a tour bus. I learned how to downsize what I needed to do a good job so that I never had to take all my massage equipment ever again. Like Merle said, all I need was hard-working hands and a good strong back, and I had both.

After several weeks on tour, I said good-bye to my life on the road with Merle and the band. I flew back home to Fairhope. He was the nicest person you could ever meet. He was as down-to-earth as you could get! I asked him one last question before I left, and that was, "Why don't you tour the deep South as much as you do the East and West Coast?" His answer was so funny, maybe he was joking when he told me that with the lifestyle he's led, he and the true Southern Baptists didn't see eye to eye on a few things he did in the past. I told him that where I come from on the Gulf Coast, his fans loved him, and he needed to come down there so we could show him our loyalty. Nowadays I have noticed that he's a regular at the casinos on the Mississippi Gulf Coast.

They flew me back to sweet home Alabama, and I couldn't wait to see Benny the Candy Man to tell him about my adventure on the road with Merle Haggard. That's when I found out that he was get married three days after he picked me up from the airport, making love at his place for two hours before he took me home to Fairhope. Life goes on, and after the break-up from Benny the Candy Man, my massage therapy business just got better and better as I worked on many more famous people.

On October 10, 1990, another newspaper article came out on the front page of the local newspaper: "Linnie Delmar Rubs Down the Movie Stars." I was mortified and embarrassed by the title! This was after I gave the associate editor who wrote the article an hour therapeutic massage just so he would know how to better write down what I really do—it is not a rubdown. Again, the reason given for why they wrote it that way was to get the attention of the people. Again, I was embarrassed and mortified, but I wasn't worried about my professional integrity getting a bad rap. Good news was on the way.

Thanks to Eva Goldson, my life was about to change for the better. She was with the Mobile Chamber of Commerce and in charge of all the movies being filmed around the Southeast. Eva was given a gift certificate to come to me when I first started my business, and after she experienced the pampering package she told me that today was my lucky day! When I asked why, she told me that all the motion-picture production companies needed someone like me. They wanted an LMT who had a different style and technique. That was the break I needed that led me to so many actors, some more famous than others. It was Eva who told them that I was the best LMT in the southeast, known as Massage Therapist to the Stars. My business was growing, and I was getting stronger as an LMT and a person. The Grand Hotel had an event they called their "Super Bowl." It was for their employees throughout the country. Awards were given to the best employees in their department at their hotel. They listed me as the best LMT for having the most unique massage technique out of all the Marriott resorts in the country. That was an unexpected feather in my cap that made by business grow as well.

The next big movie star I worked on was Steven Seagal, who in 1992 filmed the movie *Under Siege* in Mobile on the USS *Alabama* and on a soundstage at the Fairhope Airport made to look like the inside of the USS *Alabama*. His personal nutritionist, Jeff Coffman, was my contact person who hired me at Steven Seagal's request. We took all my portable equipment to set up at a charming home that Steven Seagal had rented in Point Clear for the five months that he would be filming. The house was big enough that they turned the three-car garage into a huge fitness room so that he could work out every day. The land the property was on was also big enough to have all of their favorite horses brought in all the way from California. He and his wife, Kelly LeBrock, and his children were avid, skilled horseback riders.

They allowed me to also take my baby sister Kim to help me get set up in a bedroom that we made into a spa. Kim was starstruck at first looking at Steven Seagal, but later she was able to sit down and talk to Steven for over two hours about music. Kim was the lead singer in her own band named City Limits. She had over twenty-five years of experience in music business. It thrilled me to death, and her too, that they hit it off. While they talked, I was working on Kelly LeBrock.

Kim later told me something that neither I nor a lot of people knew about this tall (six foot five), very well-built, soft-spoken man (he spoke so soft it was almost a whisper), and that was he arranged all the soundtracks for most of his movies. He played music and was a very accomplished musician. He was always very nice to me when I would go over to their house to work on him and Kelly. It seemed like every time I went over there, Steven was in the kitchen cooking; he was an excellent cook. He appeared to be an excellent husband, because he and Kelly seemed to be perfect for each other in every way. I actually worked on her more than him due to his filming schedule. She and I hit it off! She found out that I used the same kind of facial products for my clients as she used on her face. Her skin was flawless. We loved shoes and boots of all kinds, the stranger the better. When I wasn't at their house giving them the hour-long treatment, I was on the movie set with my high-touch massage chair giving mini-massages to the cast and crew.

A few times, I was in the right place at the right time, so that Steven Seagal gave me a mini-massage on the chair. I thought I had died and gone to heaven—he had great hands, the perfect touch, and the ideal technique, and he made it into art. While on the movie set, I met the actor who stole my heart, John Laughlin, and we became great friends. He came to me every day for the hour massage as well as the mini-massages. I thought he was into getting massages more than most, but really he was into me, to my surprise.

The relationship didn't go anywhere because I was dating Rich at the time. Look where that got me! I always wondered what would have happened if I had gone out with John. I guess I'll never know—that day never came. One evening while I was working late on the movie set, some of Steven Seagal's close friends and fellow actors invited me to join them for Steven's fortieth birthday party. It was a small but intimate party held at the home he was renting. I was so excited and honored to be there, but the excitement ended when I made the mistake of calling Rich to tell him where I was. I thought he would be happy for me to have an opportunity like this, but instead he was so mad at me he wanted me to leave as soon as possible. Rich was extremely jealous of the actor John Laughlin and rightfully so—John had sent me roses in an attempt to get me to date him. Of course, I never did, and wish now I had. John wasn't at the birthday party and now, looking back, if John had been at that party, the last thing I would have done was to make that stupid phone call to Rich. I missed a prime opportunity to stay at a party that I was having fun at with people I worked with every day. I proved to him that night that I was in love with him and no one else. I left the party after only being there for twenty minutes or less. I was such a fool to let a man tell me what I was going to do and not do back in those days. I'm here to tell you now, those days have been over for many years. Every memory of Steven Seagal and his wife I will cherish forever!

After working with many more actors as the years went by and my massage-therapy business was growing, the next big A-list actor that comes to mind is Gene Hackman. The first time I laid eyes on Gene Hackman was on November 24, 1998, when he was staying at Soniat House Hotel located in the French Quarter in New Orleans. He's a lot taller in person than what he appears to be on the big screen, about six foot two. He was staying in one of the private elite bungalows. As I began to quietly set up my portable massage table, I look up and there was Gene Hackman coming out of the bathroom with only a big towel wrapped around his waist. I screamed and scared the hell out of both of us. We both laughed. The first words he said to me were, "You must be Linnie-la-tur the LMT?" I told him only Linnie, because Linnie-la-tur sounds like a stripper off Bourbon Street. That sort of broke the ice, and he laughed. I asked him to fill out my information form (I require all clients to fill one out), and he said that he didn't have a pen on him because he was naked with only a towel around him. We both laughed again, and I gave him a pen. From then on, he loved calling me Linnie-la-tur, so at least that's a name he can remember. He was filming a movie in the surrounding area of New Orleans and also looking at a boat he wanted to buy. I never talk to my clients when I'm doing a massage on them. I want that to be their time to zone out, and he was no exception. After the two-hour massage was over, he assured me that any time he was in New Orleans, Ms. Linnie-la-tur was going to be the only LMT he called. He loved my unique style, and he told me it was very different from any massage he had ever had. Coming from someone who gets a massage almost every day of his life, this put me in hog heaven! Coming from Gene Hackman, it was like riding the hog all the way to heaven! He didn't talk a lot, but he did tell me that after all these years of acting, he didn't miss the glitz and glamour of Hollywood, so he lived in New Mexico. When he had a movie it was like a good paying job to him. He went to where the job site was, he did his acting, and then he went back home to his family.

I didn't see him again until the movie *Runaway Jury* was filmed in New Orleans. The date I worked on him again was November 15, 2002. I worked with him almost every day that he was filming his part in the movie. He was staying at the Ritz-Carlton on Canal Street in a huge penthouse suite. I, on the other hand, was staying with one of my best gay friends, Adam, in his charming guesthouse. I was able to walk to the Ritz-Carlton when he requested a massage.

When I wasn't working on him, I was working part-time at Classic Concepts Salon/Spa. There were times when Gene would come to me at Classic Concepts and he would ask if Linnie-la-tur was ready for him yet. If I had a client, he would sit quietly reading until it was time for his appointment. Adam and Lee said that while they were doing hair on some of their clients, the clients would look a few feet away and tell them, "Hey, do you all think that guy over there looks just like Gene Hackman?" When Adam and Lee would tell them it was him, they couldn't believe it! Lee and Adam loved the nickname he gave me, Linnie-la-tur! Gene Hackman was not only a client but now a friend, so he talked to me a lot more than he used to. He told me a great story about when he and Dustin Hoffman used to be roommates long before they were both famous. He said that they had no idea that both of them would come as far as they have. They are still the best of friends. Dustin Hoffman was also in the movie *Runaway Jury*, so every day was old home week catching up on old times together. Gene was very smart and very humble to be the living legend that he is in Hollywood. He was very laid back at times, and at times not so laid back due to the long hard hours of filming. What I remember the most is that he had the tightest hamstring muscle of anyone to date that I have ever worked on. At age seventy-two then and standing on his feet most of the day, I'm surprised that's all he had wrong with him. He was healthy and in very good shape for seventy-two, plus he was as nice and good to me as he could be. When the movie was over and I worked on him for the last time, he gave me a very generous tip, which was greatly appreciated by Ms. Linnie-la-tur!

When Geraldo Rivera would come to New Orleans, I would work on him every day he was staying at the InterContinental. I would take all my portable massage equipment to his suite and set up, then take it all down and back to Classic Concepts, where I stored it in my massage room. He didn't have an ounce of fat on him, and he was in excellent health. Unknown to most people, he is a boxer. His workout was boxing early in the morning at the New Orleans Athletic Club, then he would get his massage. He was very smart as an attorney. He was very organized as a businessman. His executive assistant would not only have his day planned out to the minute but also have his clothes laid out in perfect order. Every year when he was attending the NAPA Convention, he would invite me to be his guest. The convention was closed to the public, so I felt again like I was in the right place at the right time for attending this once-a-year event. Almost every star who was going to be on television for the next year was there. It was a sight to behold, and there I was in the middle of it all. Everyone from Regis and Kathie Lee, to Pamela Anderson, Oprah, and hundreds of other television stars were in a booth that represented the production company, and the booths were huge. The event was so huge that it had to be held at the New Orleans Convention Center. Thanks to Geraldo, I was able to make a lot of contacts for my massage business as well.

The famous author Rebecca Wells was a client who I thought would turn out to be my most difficult client (other than Mama). She would stay at the InterContinental every time she was in New Orleans for a book signing. She has written many best sellers, but my favorite is *Divine Secrets of the Ya-Ya Sisterhood*, which was later made into a movie. It has a lot of Southern humor in it, sort of like the book you are reading now. She was a tiny sassy red-headed woman who was going to tell Miss Linnie how to do her job the way she wanted it done. Of course, you know how well that went over with me. She even came into Classic Concepts with her own "music"—white noise, which I hate—but I kept my cool, as I always do with clients, and listened to all of her demands and instructions that were set in stone. In a very quiet, calm inside voice, I suggested that for the first ten minutes, we could do it my way. If she hated it or didn't like my music, I would do it her way. She was cool with that! I began my magic on her tiny firm body and within five minutes she sat up on my table and yelled out in her outside voice, "Oh my God! You know what you are doing, and I won't ever tell you what to do again, I promise!" It scared the shit out of me to say the least! From that moment on, when Mrs. Rebecca Wells and her very nice quiet husband came in for a treatment, we were the best of friends!

When the Backstreet Boys came to the Superdome to do a concert in New Orleans, they also stayed at the InterContinental. I had no clue who they were or what they did and could care less, because I had never heard any of their music. Dressed in very casual clothes, the first boy to get a massage was Brian Littrell. He had pretty blond hair and was built nice. The second boy was A.J. (Alexander James) McLean, and he looked like a sexy bad boy. He had dark hair and a goatee and was built very hard and lean. They came to me at Classic Concepts every day that they were staying in New Orleans to get a massage. They looked like kids to me because they were so young, full of personality. They both fell in love with Miss Linnie! I think because I did not care if they were famous or not. I treated them like any other clients and they loved that. They could kid around and be themselves and feel comfortable with me. They both knew how to relax and zone out because they got massages on a regular basis when they were on tour. That alone was the best compliment they could give me, because when I worked on them (of course one at a time) they fell sound asleep—music to my ears. I love it when clients can let go like that and feel like they are sinking into my soft custom massage table.

Every time they would come into the salon, a girl who worked as a nail tech named Angie would melt. She was the same age they were, and she knew the words to every song they'd recorded. The day they were to leave the hotel, she begged me to take her up to their suite so that she could get a picture with them, so I said come on. We were able to get by their bodyguards because they heard my loud voice and said, "Hey, it's Miss Linnie, please come in and join us!" Angie got her picture taken with the entire Backstreet Boys group, and so did Miss Linnie!

I met Ashley Judd while she was in New Orleans filming the movie Runaway Jury. She is not that tall and has a nice figure. She was very thin and tiny compared to how she looks on the big screen. I was surprised. She had a very soft voice and when she spoke, I could hardly hear her. She had a very gentle nature about her. She was sitting around waiting like the rest of us—I was an extra—and I began to rub her shoulders and neck and upper back. I had only been working on her for about ten minutes when she asked me if I would go get my high-touch massage chair and come back. I came back and from then on, she wanted me to do chair massages on her in between the filming of her parts in the movie. So I did! She was so nice and down to earth and loved to eat candy.

You might find these stories I have of all of these movie stars, authors, and singing groups interesting, or maybe not. The list could go on and on with more stories from actors like Brian Bosworth; soul man B.B. King; the singing group Alabama; the most famous polo player of all, Major Ronald Ferguson; and many famous people who aren't actors but are the best people at what they do.

My favorite stories don't come from famous people but from real people like me and you. In Linnie's pretend world of living the high life alongside famous people, it was more of a big deal to me far more than it was to them. In reality, I was an insignificant person to them, as were the that they would remember that stood out in their busy life. That is, except for Bill Clinton, for whom the name Linnie Delmar might ring a bell ... or maybe not. My favorite stories are the stories of regular people, hard-working people. Those are the stories dearest to my heart, and they are just as interesting and heartfelt to me as the stories you just read about the rich and the famous. One special story you will love is about a lady named Amy. It touched my heart as it will touch yours.

I had a young lady in her late thirties named Amy, very pretty and quiet, come to me several years ago. I had never worked on her before; this was her first professional massage. During the massage session, she began to cry, and I had to stop what I was doing and hand her a tissue. I asked her why she was crying. She told me that her beloved husband who was her first love and the father of their four young children had just been told that he was going to die of brain cancer. As my heart sank, and I began to tear up, I had to stop myself from completely breaking down so that I could comfort her. She told me that the massage felt so good to her that the guilt from her lying there enjoying the best thing she had ever felt was bringing her to tears.

She told me that only a few hours ago, after hearing the news about her husband, her entire life and the life of their four small children was changed forever. Her husband insisted she keep her massage appointment. What broke my heart even more was I realized it was her husband who called the day before, wanting to purchase a gift certificate for his wife.

I met him when he came by to pick up the gift certificate he had bought for her. He had also told me what time of the day to schedule her appointment. After I gave him a quick tour of the spa (the three bedrooms and one bath area in my home), he told me this place was perfect. He told me that his wife would love everything about my home/business. He asked me to do an extra special job on her because it was her first massage. I assured him that as soon as anyone walks through my front door, they start to get pampered from that moment on, up until they leave. I failed to ask him if it was a birthday gift from him or another special occasion. In most cases, that is the first question I ask a person so that I can prepare for whatever it may be, down to the last details, including the way I prepare the food. I thanked God that yesterday He stopped me from asking why he was giving her a gift certificate.

How could he tell a complete stranger that he was buying a gift certificate for his wife who will be informed tomorrow that her husband will die of brain cancer? Her husband's doctor was going to sit her down and tell her that her husband only had a very short time to live.

Using my soft massage voice, I told Amy to dry her tears, because we hadn't even got to the good stuff (techniques) yet! I also told her that her husband wanted this to be her special time. It was then that she took a deep breath, and I felt every muscle in her body let go and relax. After the massage and before Amy's husband came to pick her up, she told me that she would be back. She told me it was the only time in her life that she was so relaxed she could hardly stand up and walk when she got off the table. It was at that moment I knew, if I never do another massage on anyone ever again, working on Amy was the best massage that I had ever given to anyone in my life! It's the hundreds of stories like Amy's over the past twenty-five-plus years that keep me physically, mentally, and spiritually able to get out of bed each and every day. It's God's gift to me to allow my hands to hold up and stay strong. To do the best I can do to continue my work of helping people until the day I die!

Chapter 12

END OF MY JOURNEY

It took me a lifetime to realize that I could have a wonderful complete life being single. I love myself again as the good Christian person I have grown to become throughout the years. I know now that just because I date someone and we hit it off, that does not mean I have to marry him. That was a bad habit I had for many years, and I have learned from my mistakes not to do it again. My family, friends, and ex-husbands are still in shock that I ended up having a "big boy" in my wild life after all. He would be the key that unlocked the real me, and his name would be Harley-Davidson. It took me years of hard work to afford him. It took me a day to learn how to drive him and control the power and speed he puts between my firm thighs. It took me a lifetime to realize how simple my wants and needs were, and they have been fulfilled by something as relaxing as a motorcycle.

I have traveled around the world and ended up in my hometown of Fairhope, Alabama, of all places, and I am in love with it. I love the fact that I am sixty years old and I still have both of my parents to light up my life and visit with and have lunch with each and every day. Although they are both eighty-five years old and still live on their own, they both take turns cooking for each other and for us. Due to their strong love and affection for me, I have a beautiful home, and I am able to work out of my home, doing what I love to do. Every day I use the gift that God has blessed me with, which is pampering stressed-out people. I still have my little dog, Coco, my six-pound spoiled rotten min-pin. She is my heart and has stuck by me longer than most of my four husbands. Most of all, the real love of my life and the best gift God has blessed me with is my son, Rodney, who has always been the best of me in every way. He is smart, good-looking, strong, and proud that he is a successful gay man who loves and cherishes his life with his lifetime partner.

Most of all, though, he was not born a blue baby like his mama! He has never had to prove himself to me like I have with my mama. He still amazes me each and every day of his interesting life. I am so proud of him. He kept telling me that it doesn't take much to make me happy because I have been a happy soul from the day I was born, blue baby or not! Simple things I do, like having a good sense of humor that makes me laugh at myself, is what keeps my healthy positive attitude moving forward. The most important thing I have learned about Mama telling me that I was a blue baby was that it made me work harder to be the best I could be at whatever I did in life. I appreciate the way I learned from being the blue baby, because it made me even more special. After all, I was her first baby, blue or not. That's what made me so special my whole life. I know that, and she does, too!

Writing this book has taken years, but I am grateful for the support and encouragement from my family and from my best friends Bettie, Barbara, Theresa, Rhoda, Martha, Marcie, Sue, Valerie, Kim, Tammy Hopper, just to name a few, and let's not forget my best friend of all, Mama. I made myself stick to my goal of writing this book, and even if it's never published into a real book or even a movie, it's okay with me.

It would make a great movie, though! Of course, none other than Kathy Bates would be the perfect person to play the part of Mama. Ryan Gosling from the movie *The Notebook* or Julian McMahon from the FX-TV series *Nip/Tuck* could play Donnie, husband #1! None other than John Travolta (if he was extremely thin) with the blue eyes could play Big Al. Edward Norton would be the perfect Merle the Pearl, who was husband #2. My first choice to play husband #3 would be the actor who played Smith Jerrod in *Sex and the City*, Jason Lewis. I think he could pull that one off to play

Rich, my gay husband! Last but certainly not least would be Benicio Del Toro, the perfect man to play Tony the Pony or husband #4—they look like brothers. The best one to play me, Linnie Delmar, would be none other than the one and only Kim Cattrall from *Sex and the City*. She and I could be soul sisters because we are so much alike in so many ways when it comes to having an appreciation for good-looking men and loving sex as much as I love ice cream! Adam and Lee could just be themselves and better than any actor could do playing their parts.

Yes, in Linnie's World, these actors could play these many chapters of the sordid world I made for myself, back when I was young in my wilder days and in the present day as well. We would have a ball filming the movie in Baldwin County, God's country, Fairhope, Robertsdale, Gulf Shores, and then on to New York, Atlantic City, Las Vegas, London, Paris, Switzerland, Germany, California, Atlanta, all the places that made Miss Linnie Delmar feel famous and "divorced on the Redneck Riviera"! What can I say—it might just be a hit movie and another of many Forrest Gump moments of being in the right place at the right time. Stranger things have happened!

The good times, all the wild times, and the sad times, have made up my life, and I have lived it the only way I knew how, which was to the fullest each and every day. My motto is still "Never a dull moment" in the life of Linnie Delmar. I let every day count for something or helping someone or giving a massage to someone. Doing nice things for my mom and dad, neighbors, church family, and friends fulfills the life I have made for myself today. I love to pay it forward, and I wish everyone could pay it forward with kindness, just one kind deed a day! It could change our whole world for the better and make us better people in this stressed-out world of ours.

I loved all my husbands and lovers to the best of my ability. I learned skills of the mind to cope with them and for them to cope with me and my OCD. All along the way, it has been a learning process for all of us. If they learned nothing else from me, they know how much fun I was, what a good lover I was, and if nothing else, I was excellent entertainment for all to enjoy for years to come. When they think of me now, I know in my heart they all smile. They know I was one of a kind, and I made them laugh and get the best out of life and the life we shared together. I appreciate them for the lessons they taught me about life and how to cope with stress. I ask for their forgiveness if I ever hurt them or said bad things to them. If I hurt them it was because of my hurt from the broken heart I had from leaving them when all I ever wanted was one good man who wanted me and would tell me, "Linnie, you're the one."

I appreciate my close family always being there for me to lean on during the good times and the bad. God love them for what they have put up with throughout the years—especially in my young years when I was buck wild and sex ruled my world living life to the fullest on the Redneck Riviera. They kept an open mind when I would share with them what really went on in my world. I told them things they really did not want to know and should have been left unsaid. I did not let them into Linnie's World too often, but when they came to visit that wild side, they did not seem to be surprised. They have always told me that I am in a league of my own and ahead of my time, with the nerve of Dick Tracy, whatever the hell that means. I am the first to realize that with all the places I have been and all the people I have met along the way, I have lived in a safe bubble of life that I can't explain other than being in the right place at the right time. I pray in my older years that safe bubble of life will take me to new places to meet new people and will not pop until God is ready for it to.

I ask God sometimes, why me? Why did I have four husbands: a workaholic, an alcoholic, a gay man, and an actor/prescription-drug addict hooked on pain pills? All of them were eye candy and hung like a horse on steroids—tall, good-looking men you would see in *GQ* or *Playgirl* magazines. All of them fell in love with me, and they all loved me like sugar. Why did I not choose and have an open mind and not be so shallow to meet a normal man of normal size and shape? How did I, with only a high-school education, get to travel with millionaires around the world and never make a lot of money in my entire life? How did I put myself in places where I became known as Massage Therapist to the Stars? I also participated in some movies with A-list actors standing next to me (as an extra) in cities like New Orleans, Hollywood, London, and Paris, just to mention a few. When some people looked at me in my younger years, they really thought I was from Hollywood, California. Then when I opened my big mouth, they heard this loud Southern hick voice come out of me and knew I was a country-ass girl from Fairhope, Alabama, and proud of it! I have seen it all, done it all, and I have had so many fun adventures along the way. Just like being the female version of Forrest Gump, being in the right place at the right time.

All I know is now I can truly say I can see the big picture and listen to the signs that God gives us when that little voice inside of us is speaking loud and clear. I hear it now! When I was young, I would ignore that little voice and let sex rule me because it was my drug of choice at the time. It would take over my mind and body before I could think clearly and see the light. I have loved so deeply at times that my body was physically sick when that love was over and done with. I have lost loves of my life by bad timing and having no common sense. I have said good-bye to the love of my life by not giving into my self-esteem and for having too much pride to say, "I want you back." After leaving, all I wanted to do was go back and say I'm sorry and ask for things to be back to the way they were. I have tasted and smelled raw lust to the point I let it take over. Not seeing how it was the love and the need to be intimate with my mates that I needed as much as the lust of down and dirty raw sex.

I have come full circle from Robertsdale to Fairhope, to Pensacola back to Fairhope, to Gulf Shores back to Fairhope, to New Orleans to Atlanta, and now finally back home to Fairhope and the Redneck Riviera. What a ride it was all along the way, having to start my life over and over and over again. Now I am free to come and go and do whatever I want to do whenever I want to do it. I'm a strong independent woman and on my own. I have the love of my son, Rodney, and my Mama and Dad and my two sisters and lots and lots of close friends. With Coco by my side and Big Boy sitting polished up in my garage wanting me to hop on him at any given time, to ride like the wind. My journey has been living my life, and I think I have done a pretty good job along the way.

I see myself years from now still being the owner of my quaint little day spa in Fairhope, Alabama, working out of my home as long as my strong little hands hold up for me. Still being the famous Massage Therapist to the Stars ... and anyone else who wants to feel like the most special person in the world by getting the relaxing experience of my unique one-of-a-kind massage. I see myself happy that I can still use the gift God gave me to please and pamper people, because I love my job and I love people. I see myself teaching my technique to LMTs who want to own their own business.

I also see myself staying strong with the free spirit and fun sense of humor I was born with, sharing myself with my special friend Larry. I wrote this book, lived this life of mine the way I saw it through the eyes of Linnie's World! I had many loves along the way in my favorite place of all, the Redneck Riviera. It's not over yet, but we'll see what life after sixty brings as God keeps and protects me in His hands and in the light of life that He continues to provide for me that leads my way and lights my path each and every day of my fun-filled life!

Ladies who are reading this book right now, I'll give you some advice. Remember, this advice is coming from the voice of experience. I have had four husbands (eye candy from the word go and dicks the size of Texas), and I have had more lovers than I want to count. The best word to describe a man is "testosterone." The reason I can say that is because after my complete hysterectomy, I had to start taking a small dose of testosterone. When I say it is a small dose, I mean it is a dose about the size of a mole on a gnat's ass. That tiny dose has shot my libido to the moon. My boyfriend will ask every few months, "Is it time for your shot?" over and over again.

When you hear experts say that men think of sex every six seconds, believe them! It hit me like a ton of bricks after I started taking that tiny dose of testosterone, because I figured out why men love sex and have to have it all the time, why they cheat, and most of all why they have no clue why we are so different from them. They carry around sacks full of testosterone all the time—their balls. Don't get mad at them, because that is the way God made them, and they can't help it. The honest truth is so simple: men have balls and we don't! Although sometimes we think we do when times are hard and the strong women of the world have to step up to the plate. We have their babies, we put up with God knows what just to make them happy, we will go to the ends of the world to love them and take care of them, and we will even wax their bass boat for them—but we will never have balls, no matter how big the shot is!

End of story!

LaVergne, TN USA
28 September 2010
198802LV00003B/1/P